How the English *Created* CANADA

An Intriguing History of Explorers, Rogues, Fur Traders, Pioneers, Prime Ministers, Heroes and Scoundrels

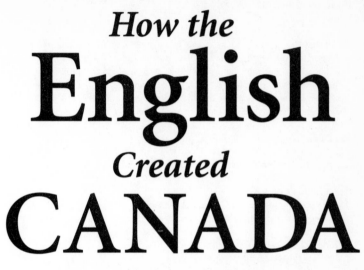

How the English *Created* CANADA

An Intriguing History of
Explorers, Rogues, Fur Traders,
Pioneers, Prime Ministers,
Heroes and Scoundrels

JEFF PEARCE

DRAGON
HILL

© 2008 by Dragon Hill Publishing Ltd.
First printed in 2008 10 9 8 7 6 5 4 3 2 1
Printed in Canada

The Publisher: Dragon Hill Publishing Ltd.

Library and Archives Canada Cataloguing in Publication

Pearce, Jeff, 1963–
    How the English created Canada : An intriguing history of explorers, rogues, fur traders, pioneers, prime ministers, heroes and scoundrels / Jeff Pearce.

Includes bibliographical references.
ISBN 978-1-896124-20-9

    1. English—Canada—History.   2. Canada—Civilization—English influences.   3. Canada—History. I. Title.

FC106.B7P42 2009   971.0042'1   C2008-908092-0

Project Director: Gary Whyte
Project Editor: Gary Whyte

Cover Images: Jupiterimages Corporation

Photography and Illustration credits: Every effort has been made to accurately credit the sources of photographs and illustrations. Any errors or omissions should be directed to the publisher for changes in future editions. Photography and illustrations courtesy of Archives of Ontario (p. 83, Major General Sir Isaac Brock, by George Theodore Berthon, 694158); Canton, E. Thomas (p. 76; p. 240); Library of Congress (chapter opening throughout, USZ62-3018; p. 29, USZ62-46032; p. 37, USZ62-45335; p. 45, USZ62-47; p. 147, DIG-ppmsca-08560); Wikimedia Commons (from Collection of Euston Hall, Suffolk {{PD-Art}}, p19); Wikimedia Commons (from Library and Archives Canada {{PD-Canada}}, p. 168); The Yorck Project: *10,000 Meisterwerke der Malerei,* Zenodot Verlagsgesellschaft mbH (p. 55).

We acknowledge the support of the Alberta Foundation for the Arts for our publishing program.

PC: P5

CONTENTS

DEDICATION

For Blair on the Home Front, and also for those in
England: Sam, Steve my drinking hero and the slacker
supreme, the ever-reliable Maria and Ruben,
Debunker of Myths, Keeper of Al-Kebulan Honour
in the midst of pale, dour barbarians.

But most of all, for my beloved daughter, Lily.

Acknowledgements

I would like to thank several individuals without whose help this book would not have been possible: Gary Whyte at Dragon Hill, Blair Cosgrove for his insightful suggestions, Tom Canton for recommendations and his unapologetic Brock worship and Professor William Tetley, who was so gracious in his correspondence with me and whose book was an invaluable source text. The reader should understand that my conclusions and any errors are mine alone.

INTRODUCTION

D uring my childhood, my father—who never set foot off the continent of North America his entire life—had the habit of calling an umbrella a "brolly." When I was a little boy, my mother still kept the habit of serving tea at four in the afternoon (one that for all my interests in things English, I never did quite pick up in adulthood). Folks in Winnipeg, where I was born, didn't go to a bar—they went round to the *pub* (I didn't hear anyone call a watering hole a "bar" until I moved to Toronto). At school, we sang "God Save the Queen" just as routinely as we sang "O Canada" (with the original, secular lyrics before someone got the idea that God should be invoked to hold the country together). And when I was a little older, I went to *Earl Grey* Junior High School.

There were touchstones of British—and often more specifically English—culture all around me, so much so that I suspect mine was the last generation to grow up steeped in this Anglophile atmosphere. The connection was still strong enough that when I entered a public-speaking competition at that same Earl Grey Junior High School with the resolution that Canada didn't need the monarchy anymore, I infuriated the contest judges. I have forgotten many of the details of this little storm of controversy, but I will never forget looking down from the podium on the gym stage at a glowering man seated behind a long table. Adults wiser and more sophisticated than me agreed that I'd been made a political example, and the principal, who went so far as to apologize to me personally, saw to it that I got into the advancing round through some loophole in the rules. If, at the age of 15, I didn't want to follow God's example and save the Queen, there were certainly others in Canada who did.

These memories came to mind when I started to write this book. In one of the previous volumes in this series, *How the Italians Created Canada*, Josie Andrews-Di Sciascio describes her immigrating to Canada from the Old Country, and I realized that mine is also, in a way, an immigrant's journey—only one done in reverse.

I first visited England in my early twenties, getting my chance to see the teeming metropolis of London months before I ever set foot on Toronto's Yonge Street. The stern male voice at the time on the Tube (it's now been changed to a more comforting feminine one) warned me to "Mind the Gap," and Thatcher's England was a grim, grey place where the Stock Market was opened up to Americans but thousands of English felt alienated by Draconian policies and Reagan-style economics.

I was hopelessly, ridiculously naïve, thinking I was *of* these people with all the hand-me-down affectations of English culture I had inherited from my family and my hometown of Winnipeg. I was nothing of the kind. Yes, I was a tall, white male with blue eyes and (back then) a full head of blond hair, who got stopped on the street again and again by other tourists because I could be mistaken for English. That was as far as it went; I was something else. You are never quite so defined in terms of nationality as when you're in a foreign setting. So I feel that my own personal struggle in coming to terms with my English heritage reflects the similar challenge faced by many other Canadians.

I make no claim to discovering anything new, but then this is not a book for academics. There will be gaps and different emphases placed in the narrative than in general surveys of Canadian history. I haven't paid much attention to explorers because, frankly, *finding* something is less important than *keeping* it when we're talking about what made Canada what it is today. Whole books have been written on the individual chapter themes, and this book has to compress more than 300 years of history.

We can start by considering the very specific title of this slim volume. It is *How the English Created Canada*—not how the "British" helped found the country. In a bygone age, it was true that to use the term "British" was almost synonymous in a casual if somewhat lazy way with "English" when talking of values or even about culture. People knew what you meant. Today, you interchange those words at your peril in the company of any proud Scot, Welsh or even Northern Irish citizen, who will be all too happy to correct you—and maybe pour a drink over your head. To be English today in Britain implies *descent*, and given the number of African and Afro-Caribbean, Indian and Asian immigrants to the UK after the World War II, the term obviously won't cut it. But the truth is the words "Britain" and "British" have always been political conceits.

In fact, the concept of what it means to be "English" has become so blurred over the decades of the last century and during this new one that Jeremy Paxman decided to explore it in a wonderful book, naturally entitled *The English*. Paxman is not a household name in Canada, but in Britain he's a famous journalist and interrogator on *NewsNight* (fiercer and less polite than Mike Wallace could ever dream of) who strikes fear into the hearts of contestants as the host of *University Challenge*, a show that Canada's own high school version, *Reach for the Top*, probably owed a lot of inspiration.

Paxman notes how, since the English dominated the British imperial machine, "English" became a synonym for "British." He reminds us, "Walter Bagehot's monumental work on the relationship between Parliament, the crown and the courts of the United Kingdom—still the classic introduction to the subject, despite being over 100 years old—is called *The English Constitution*. In the 1920s, Andrew Bonar Law, a Canadian of Scots-Ulster descent, and therefore, one might have thought, sensitive about these things, was happy to be called 'Prime Minister of England.'"

Paxman makes a persuasive case that being "English" has always been and still is a state of mind, and in English Canada we've inherited values from them—both grand and subtle—characteristics that can be amusingly familiar. For instance, Paxman writes about the peculiar romanticism the English have for the countryside, a nostalgia for a pastoral nirvana that only briefly, if ever, existed. And who does that sound like? English Canadians constantly talk about "going to the cottage" or "heading up to the lake" (it's always *the* lake, as if there's only one), yet most of us now live in urban settings. We talk big about worshipping Nature, but few of us stay in the woods. If we were honest with ourselves, we'd admit that our culture is urban-driven, created in urban centres, and has been for decades.

He also writes how one of the defining characteristics of English people is their sense of privacy. "Unlike some other countries, where casual socializing can take place in the home, the English have a very protective sense of their hearth and prefer the restaurant or pub."

Who does that sound like? My foreign friends routinely complain that, in cities like Toronto or Calgary, it's hard to *break in*, to get to know people. And years ago, a poll discovered that as a people, we prefer to drive to work alone.

By the time I moved to England around the turn of the millennium (I was following a beautiful woman back home, which was as good a reason as any), Paxman's book was already out in paperback. I recognized similarities between Canadians and the English but was also jarred by our differences. England today is a land of anachronisms, where the English might rush off for a healthy "takeaway" from an Indian restaurant and yet complain minutes later about "all these immigrants." I personally believe England's parliamentary system and tradition of laws is one of the true wellsprings of modern democracy, with a little too much credit given without challenge to tax-dodging, slave-owning landowners of the Thirteen Colonies. And yet in post-war, post-punk London, when I was a financial magazine editor on my way to meet with a member of the editorial board at his home in Kensington, I was pulled aside by the advertising manager who whispered, "Now be sure you address him as *Sir* Michael…."

Reared in a country where everybody thinks they're middle class even when they're not, I made sure I did nothing of the kind. To his credit, the "Sir Michael" in question, as the English say, didn't give a toss whether he was called Michael or Mister.

So it's useful to consider what England has become—and we'll return to this in the last chapter—because I would argue that by aspiring in values to be an England that only existed in the poems of Kipling and jingoistic editorials of London newspapers, Canada re-invented itself from a colonial holding into something unique and lasting, the legitimate heir of those values.

If fair-mindedness, tolerance, polite decorum and a resourceful sense of humour were once traits assigned to the English (and ones the English assigned to themselves), where do we find them today? They're found in a country that accepted the concept of gay marriage, that welcomes thousands of immigrants each year, that has citizens famous around the world for having manners to the point where travelling Americans disguise themselves with our flag, and that has comedic talent we actually export to become superstars south of the border.

Is this almost relentlessly pleasant image just an existential wish? No. Consider this observation made as late as 1995 by military historian, John Keegan. Despite being born to an Irish Catholic family, Keegan is about as British as you can get—he lectured at Sandhurst and for the BBC, he was awarded the OBE (Order of the British Empire to you, mate), and he was born in Clapham to boot (nice place if you can afford it, and if you like being smack dab in the middle of London's commuter belt). Canada, wrote Keegan,

is, underneath the North American accent and stripped of the superficialities of American cars, architecture and clothes, a very English country...a sort of Atlantic New Zealand in its concern for social welfare, legal propriety, electoral equality, and women's rights.... With a little exposure, the British can feel quite at home in Canada, and those who make the transition find themselves quick—as I am—to rebut the lazy judgment that it is dull or provincial or imitative or characterless.

All this brings us to a set of political baggage that comes out of historical revisionism, the kind that's out-lived both its stay and its usefulness. ✓

Today many young people and teenagers in Canadian schools are taught and, indeed, parrot a deliberate polit-ical amnesia. It is the fiction that we "are a nation of immigrants." In so far as recent history goes and look-ing at developing trends, yes, of course, that's true up to a point. A country has to evolve, and we are richer for those who come from abroad and bring something fresh to the table. We are mostly a nation of immigrants today because there has never been so many before, and we should be glad for it.

But there's also a note of self-congratulatory arrogance in this assertion. It says "My, aren't we fair! We're not at all like what *they* used to be—we can simply redefine ourselves to set us apart." It allies us with the more com-fortable recent image we have of ourselves as peacekeepers and gets us off the hook for being anything remotely like one of those *other* countries that has an embarrassing colonial past—that waged wars to hang onto valuable real estate such as Algeria, South Africa, Congo and Vietnam. History will go away if you ignore it long enough, but it has a habit of coming back and knocking on the door like a bill collector.

There is much English Canada has to answer for, and we'll explore that, and yet there is also much for us to celebrate. Erasing or diminishing this heritage is to ignore what we were, which means we cannot know who we truly are. As much as the English came and pillaged and took what they wanted in building their empire, there is not a nation on earth, including the aboriginal ones, that didn't have wars of conquests. Scratch a descendant of any people, and you will find a war crime in their ethnicity. I don't need to be an apologist for, or be embarrassed by, English attacks on the French or the ones on the aboriginal peoples—any more than Ms. Andrews-Di Sciascio need ever feel she has to call me up and give an explanation why her ancestors beat up mine near Hadrian's Wall when the Roman legions showed up. What *is* needed is acknowledgement of history as it happened, a full accounting of what was done and the underlying motives.

So when it comes down to it, I am not an immigrant—I was born in Winnipeg in 1963. My father was not an immigrant either, born in the same city. And that brings us full circle back to the journey. At what point am I, or anyone else for that matter, allowed to stake a claim in my own nation and call myself *of* this country? The "all immigrants" theory has to be discarded. When you extrapolate it to its absurd conclusion in logic, it's insulting not only to those of English descent born here, but every fourth generation black Canadian in Nova Scotia whose ancestors fought with the Loyalists and every proud Québecois who can trace his or her family back to Montcalm's army. If we all call ourselves immigrants, we reject both the rich heritage of those who came before—their triumphs as well as their injustices and excesses—and worse, we ignore the responsibility for a shared view of citizenship, what they used to call "Civics." One can be proud of heritage while acknowledging the truth of what happened.

Part of that Canadian heritage belongs to my daughter, Lily, a mixed race child whose mother is British of proud Jamaican roots. My daughter's great-grandfather, Charles Pearce, was an English hairdresser for the Eaton's store on Winnipeg's Portage Avenue, who moved to the "Gateway to the West" in Canada from Stratford-upon-Avon with his Birmingham bride. Lily is a beautiful product of at least three cultures. And I hope one day she will see the beauty and wonder of this still-young country as I see it, with the amazing contribution made by one of the founding peoples whose blood flows through her own, as it flows through mine.

COLD COMFORTS

Thecoma portrait in the left-hand corner shows an austere regal figure, his head covered in black curls, the image itself framed by a large "C" that helps to spell out *Charles the Second* in big bold letters above tiny writing, amid all the flourishes and decorations on the paper. For decades and maybe still today, every school child under 12 in Canada saw this image in a photo of a history textbook—it's the first page of the charter for the Hudson's Bay Company.

Kids are told a king, this particular king by the way (whoever he was), signed off on this document that you can never actually read in the photo and that things finally got rolling in this country with the fur trade. Turn the page.

The bigger picture was always much more interesting. First of all, the king in the portrait was anything but austere. Before Charles II helped open a vast stretch of Canada, he brought his own country out of the cold.

Charles was only nine years on the throne when he gave his royal assent to one of Canada's most famous documents, and England was still recovering from Cromwell's Puritans, who could give the Khmer Rouge and the Taliban a run for their money. Cromwell's armies had massacred enough Irish and Scots for his name to be hated in both regions for generations after, and in England itself. He had set up a theocracy where there was no dancing, no plays, very little music and simply going for a walk on a Sunday had better include a church as your final destination. Cromwell was so loathed in the end that his corpse was stolen from Westminster Abbey, hanged in chains at Tyburn and tossed into a pit while his head was stuck on a pole outside the Abbey for 20 years. You have to be quite steamed to want to kill a fellow after he's already dead.

With the Restoration, England opened its lungs, desperate to breathe in culture, which had almost been completely extinguished—and commerce. It started to look again beyond its own shores.

Up until this time, English forays into Canada hadn't been very impressive. Those same history textbooks tell us about John Cabot landing at Newfoundland for Henry the VII in 1497, finding the land that God supposedly "gave to Cain." But Cabot was actually Giovanni Caboto, and his accomplishments hardly count as English ones. Queen Elizabeth I sent Martin Frobisher off to find the Northwest Passage. He didn't. On his third voyage, the crew of one of his ships decided they would rather be back in England, while another ship, carrying the lumber needed to build a colony, sank. Worse, Frobisher brought more than

1000 tonnes of ore back home that turned out to be fool's gold. In 1610, Henry Hudson tried to find China and wound up set adrift by mutineers in a row-boat with only his son and a handful of loyal crew-members. While his name is still attached to the great bay and to Hudson Strait, he paid the ultimate price for his failure to find the Pacific Ocean.

Charles II of England in the robes of the Order of the Garter, c. 1675

During all this time, of course, Samuel de Champlain was solidifying things in New France, crossing the Atlantic again and again, and the Spanish had already slaughtered thousands of Aztecs in Mexico, swept aside the Inca Empire in Peru and were still the colonial superpower to beat. The English were coming late to the table, with pitifully few pins on that vague mass of North America. Given their record so far, it's hard to see why any ruler should stake a fresh expedition.

But this was the New World in more ways than one for England, with a new ruler who saw things differently and patronized both the arts and the sciences. You can stroll around London today and conduct your own walking tour based on the single theme of how much his reign had an impact. Only months after he came to power, the Royal Society, which he helped found, was off and running with meetings at Gresham College in Bishopsgate and boasting members such as Sir Isaac Newton and Sir Christopher Wren (who would be kept busy rebuilding the capital after the Great Fire). Charles founded a home for retired soldiers, the Royal Hospital, Chelsea, still housing veterans today. Tiny Soho Square, just off Tottenham Court Road—where dozens of people stretch out on its lawns every summer—still has his statue. And if you use your imagination, you can probably picture the whorehouses frequented by his courtiers in Covent Garden.

That's because Charles II was the *party king*. As grim and relentlessly humourless as the Puritans had been, Charles was the living embodiment of the pendulum swinging the other way. He had an open contempt for court ceremony (which pretty much set the tone for the rest of the court), and he liked gambling, drinking and sex. He liked them a lot. In the cluttered chaos of the massive Palace of Whitehall (this version would burn down in 1698), he never lacked for company. Courtiers, whores, hangers-on, ambassadors, servants, officials—they sometimes had legitimate business, often not. Charles somehow managed to find the time for 39 mistresses. Unlike Cromwell, the man who put his father off his throne and off his head, Charles did have a sense of humour. He commissioned an artist to paint one of his lovers, the Duchess of Cleveland, plus the illegitimate son he had with her, as a Madonna and child (incidentally, a descendant of that cherub in the portrait was Diana, Princess of Wales).

What the king didn't know was how to live within a budget. He gave Dunkirk back to the French simply to collect £400,000, and Samuel Pepys, whose diaries tell us so much of what was going on at the time, complained in 1666 that the king's musicians were "ready to starve," they were so behind in back pay.

It's worth pausing to consider what type of man Charles was because he turned out to be the best sponsoring monarch a couple of explorers could hope to meet. Consider for a moment that you are Charles Stuart. Your nation is still licking its wounds from a civil war, and everyone else in Europe thinks your countrymen are crazy. After all, they beheaded their own king and replaced him with… well, a kind of king-like leader until that one died, replaced by Cromwell's son, and then things broke down. And these English outlawed dancing—*dancing*, can you believe it? Europe, in fact, already thinks your people are a rather uncivilized lot to begin with, and everyone *knows* the finest literature, art and music all come from France. Since you spent part of your exile there, you are fairly sure of it, too.

And let us never forget, your home *is an island*. Doubt-less, Charles never did. If the English people couldn't grow it or trade it at home, they had to look elsewhere, and England's nearest neighbour and frequent enemy right across the Channel was a whole lot bigger. After years of upheaval, the land needed new "revenue streams," to use today's business jargon—it needed all it could get. Yes, there was already the East India Company, which had been expanding its trading posts, but it needed some attention as well (and Charles soon gave that operation in India sweeping powers, including the power to mint money).

So he was in a listening mood when someone came along with an opportunity. But Charles wasn't a foolish gambler. The explorers who were granted an audience with him weren't English at all, but French—they were from a people that had already proven their exper-tise in opening routes within the New World. In fact, the only reason why they were knocking on this king's door was because they were given the bum's rush by their own people.

Pierre-Esprit Radisson and his older brother-in-law Médard Chouart Des Groseilliers were two mavericks eager to strike it rich in lands beyond the secure frontiers of New France. Radisson had been captured as a teenager by Iroquois and had endured grisly tortures, managing to escape and not lose his dreams, while Groseilliers wanted to find out if the stories he heard were true about beaver ponds just *waiting* to be exploited beyond Lake Superior. In 1659, the pair went to the governor, the Marquis d'Argenson, and offered to go explore the remote unknown "for the good of the country" (and the good, of course, of Radisson and Groseilliers).

The governor listened to all this and replied to the effect of "Boys, that sounds good, here's the deal. You can go, but you'll take along a couple of government officials, and when you get back, *we* collect half the profits." Radisson and Groseilliers balked at the terms. They were, after all, taking all of the risk, and Radisson knew better than anyone else the dangers involved, especially with Iroquois determined to keep the fur trapping regions out of white European encroachment. If Radisson's account is to be believed, his brother-in-law told the governor a slightly more eloquent French version of "Get stuffed." Their pitch session disintegrated so badly that at the end, the governor outright barred them from going at all.

They went anyway. The two left in the dead of night, paddling up the Ottawa River, and the short version is that yes, they made it eventually to Lake Superior, made friends with Ojibwa, survived famine, survived a battle with the Iroquois and came back to Montréal with a fleet of canoes stuffed with fur pelts. You'd think there was a happy ending. But then as now, bureaucrats do not like being defied, and they hate even more being proved wrong. When the expedition was first discussed, the Marquis wanted half the pelts; now he wanted most of them. He fined the pair for trading without a licence and let Groseilliers cool his heels in jail for a while.

There is no other way to see the governor's actions as anything but myopic. A wealth of pelts had sailed down the river, and instead of recognizing the potential for expansion the governor must have worried that the already dwindling fur trade around the St. Lawrence—his turf—could be put out of business. Now he alienated the two experienced adventurers who knew the way and had secured alliances with the Natives in the region.

So you can't really blame Radisson and Groseilliers for packing up and heading off to Boston, where they hoped to find a more enlightened and appreciative backer. What they found was a valuable contact, a Colonel George Cartwright on a tax-collecting mission in New England, who persuaded the pair to return with him to London.

Radisson and Groseilliers made it there in 1665, the year London was ravaged by bubonic plague. Poorly paid nurses robbed the dead, which numbered in the dozens per week, and at night there were multiple glows of torches of the constantly busy gravediggers. The city would become such a ghost town that grass grew in the main street of Whitehall Palace. The King wasn't there to see it—he had wisely shifted his court to Oxford and didn't come back to Whitehall until February of the next year. Radisson and Groseilliers finally got their royal audience in late October, where they must have made an impression on Charles. The king gave them royal protection and a weekly pension of 40 shillings. And he got them talking to his cousin, Prince Rupert.

Like the portrait of Charles on the charter, Rupert was always more interesting than just being the namesake for Rupert's Land. He fought in both cavalry units and at sea for Charles I and for his cousin, and he was a gifted scientific dilettante, crafting designs for early torpedoes and revolvers and even coming up with new surgical instruments in the hopes he could get an operation to save him from horrible migraines. Rupert was the one who sweet-talked investors into financing an expedition, so that this pair of Frenchmen could explore Hudson Bay and divert a wealth of fur pelts away from New France into England's hands.

As with any corporate launch or carefully staged media event today, Rupert made sure the Money got to see what it was paying for. After a celebratory banquet, the investors took rowboats down the Thames to the major port of Gravesend (today it's a pleasant little shopping town and is still the headquarters of the Port of London Authority Thames Navigation Service). They had come to watch two ships be towed out to sea, and on June 3, 1668, Radisson was saying goodbye to the coast of England aboard the *Eaglet*, while Groseilliers was on the *Nonsuch*. They were on their way to Canada.

The *Eaglet*, however, had to limp its way back to Gravesend after a storm. It was the *Nonsuch* that completed the inaugural journey, and considering the ship itself, this must have been an amazing feat. You get a true sense of the scale of the vessel (with a length that spans only 16 metres) if you stop into an exhibit at Manitoba's Museum of Man and Nature in Winnipeg. This was the last stop ever of a replica made by the Hudson's Bay Company to mark the company's 300th birthday in 1970. As a child, I used to walk up and down that main deck on many a weekend, and even to a 10-year-old the *Nonsuch* seemed tiny.

But when Prince Rupert's ship literally came in, it delivered—there were pelts aplenty. After expenses and customs duties, plus the fact that the *Eaglet* was a bust, the expedition actually couldn't show a profit. Who cared? That didn't matter to the prince or the other backers, and when you consider there were always high odds that both ships could be lost or possibly return with nothing, you can appreciate their optimism. A new ship—this time a more substantial frigate—was constructed for what was expected to be an ongoing lucrative trade, and the investors went around London sporting £34 fur hats.

That brings us full circle to that document with that portrait of Charles II in the history books. For, as much as they banged on about the fur trade in history classes in grade school, the real accomplishment of the 1670 charter was *land*.

Rupert's Land—which divided up Canada according to the waters draining into Hudson Bay—spanned a whopping 4,000,000 square kilometres and took in all of Manitoba with great big chunks of the Northwest Territories, Nunavut, Saskatchewan, Alberta, Ontario, Québec and even pieces of what is today's northern United States.

There is a wonderful exchange in James Clavell's novel, *Shogun*, in which the hero, Blackthorne, explains to the Japanese warlord Toranaga how the kings of Spain and Portugal split the ownership of the New World. Toranaga, ever the pragmatic ruler, replies that this is nonsense, and that he "could equally well split the world between himself and the Emperor of China."

But this was, of course, exactly how things were done in Europe in 1670, and the fact that Radisson, Groseilliers, Rupert and even Charles himself were well aware that aboriginal peoples were already on this land mattered nothing. Charles just had to worry whether Louis XIV of France would take offence, since he had handed out his own charter to a Dutch navigator in the same year.

From here on, Radisson and Groseilliers are no longer main actors on our stage. They worked for the Hudson's Bay Company (HBC) for a mere five years, and never driven by loyalty to company or nationality, they went back to New France (Radisson even led a raid for the French on the HBC trading post at Port Nelson—and then later switched sides again to the English). Meanwhile, back in London, Prince Rupert, as the first HBC governor, was arranging tax breaks through his royal cousin and using his friend, the Earl of Shaftesbury, to campaign for a stipend for himself at the regular meeting of the Company's investors. After only a dozen years, the Hudson's Bay Company was generating an annual profit of 200 percent return on invested capital.

At this point in our story, it's looking more like "How Canada Created England"—all that wonderful money piling up as a cushion under the seat of empire. This is why we don't really need to follow the Hudson's Bay Company anymore for a while; its progress from here on is mostly a *corporate* history.

True, those who first sat on the company board were members of the king's own Privy Council. When the Duke of Marlborough took over as the Company's governor, he arranged for Royal Navy ships to guard HBC territory. The French—realizing they were losing ground in North America—conducted raids on trading posts and fought skirmishes with the English over the next few years. Did any of this matter? Did all this fighting have a lasting impact on Canada? Not one bit.

Yes, the English were trapping and trading in Rupert's Land, but their trading posts were changing England's economy more than they were changing Canada, and you don't get points in the measure of civilization for just showing up and sticking around.

The HBC wasn't there for civilization; it was there for money. Quite soon, the Company recognized that its interests weren't always the same as those of England. Its board members liked to cook the books every so often, and as we'll find out much later on, the Company wasn't above outright lying to the British government when this served its interests. Anyone who ever gets misty-eyed with patriotism over the Hudson's Bay Company as a "Canadian institution" only has to read about its jealous guarding of its own interests as Canada developed. It takes a little bit of the bite out of the knowledge that the HBC is now no longer Canadian-owned.

No, what drove the English to start creating Canada was the rising tension between New France and the colonies to the south in New England and New York. This is where the English had come in great numbers. It's one thing to have pelts arrive on a ship from an obscure trading post, as lucrative as those pelts are, and quite another to have ongoing traffic and tax revenue and voices from growing populations.

After little wars that didn't get either the British or the French very much, British ships arrived in force in 1710. A siege was laid on Port Royal, and France's king at the time, Louis XIV, sued for peace. His country was bankrupt, and war was expensive. Part of the terms of the peace treaty signed at Utrecht in Holland in 1713 meant France gave up trying to take any of the Hudson's Bay Company posts. This is another reason why we part ways with the HBC for a long while. No foreign power, including France, ever made a serious effort to go after the Company's turf again.

What the English also brought away from the peace deal at Utrecht was substantial mastery of the sea-lanes and territories in the Maritimes. The French got to keep Isle St. Jean—what we now call Prince Edward Island. They also kept Ile Royale, Cape Breton, though amazingly, they were ready at first to part with it (which is odd, because if they had, their ships would have had to face a gauntlet of British Maritime islands and forts to reach New France). The English got Newfoundland and "all of Nova Scotia or Acadia."

The acquisition of Nova Scotia made the English very happy. As early as 1658, well before Charles II was signing over Rupert's Land to the so-called Company of Adventurers, the English thought it might be a great idea if they forced any French there to pack up and go elsewhere.

View from the Bay of Fundy: "The Isle Haut, bearing N.b.W. distant 4 miles and Cape Chignecto, N.N.E. 3 leagues"

The French settlers—the Acadians—were minding their own business. They fished, they farmed, and they had built lasting relations and intermarried with the native Mi'kmaq. Both the English and French were suspicious of the Acadians, and the governor of New France, Louis de Baude Frontenac, considered them downright "parliamentary" in the way they traded and fraternized with folks from Massachusetts. Acadie had been captured and swapped back before. The Acadians had become such pawns in the chess game—first under the flag of France, then under the control of England, then France and now England again—that even the English had taken to calling them "neutrals."

In 1713, when Acadie was ceded to the English, an oath of allegiance was demanded from all these inconvenient and stubbornly independent French Catholics. Forget it, the Acadians told the governor of Port Royal (which the English called Annapolis-Royal). "When our ancestors lived under English domination, they were never required to take such an oath."

In 1722, the Irish lieutenant-governor, Lawrence Armstrong, won a critical concession. He managed to talk the Acadians into swearing a loyalty oath that exempted them from fighting for the British. The strategy was to win ground by inches, to "get them over by degrees" as Armstrong put it. As historian Dean Jobb points out, it looks like he never cleared this with London, and five years later he tried to get a new oath, one with military obligations. Forget it, the Acadians told him.

Back in London, the English decided the best way to secure Nova Scotia would be to, well...fill it up with more English. So in 1748, the Duke of Bedford wrote up a plan for an ambitious new settlement to be located on Chebucto Bay. Another big brain behind this scheme was the governor of Massachusetts, who was disgusted that the fort of Louisbourg had been so graciously but impractically returned to the French after the last war. To him, it was the Sword of Damocles hanging down over his colony in America.

Bedford did a hard sell to Cabinet, arguing that the new settlement would ensure "the security of the northern colonies and the preservation of Her Majesty's Dominions in America." This is how we got Halifax, founded in 1749.

The man in charge of making it happen was young Edward Cornwallis. He would wind up hating his job. For one thing, the simple English peasants who sailed over weren't disciplined like soldiers and didn't show up to build fortifications when they were ordered. It took a lottery for formal land allocations to motivate the colonists and bring them to heel. Tensions and conflicts mounted with the Mi'kmaq, who didn't take kindly to the arrogant newcomers encroaching on their domain, and the governor's solution was to fight instead of learning ways to co-exist with them as the French had.

Cornwallis demanded a loyalty oath from the Acadians as well. Forget it, they told Cornwallis. By now you see the pattern emerging.

Someone dreamed up the idea of importing German Protestant settlers as a ham-fisted tactic to get the Acadians to assimilate. All that did was further provoke the Mi'kmaq, and the "Foreign Protestants" moved off and wound up building nearby Lunenburg. The tab grew higher and higher to defend Nova Scotia as a British domain, and Cornwallis finally had enough and went home to England in 1752.

The Acadians would get stuck with someone far worse. Charles Lawrence, having served as an officer under Cornwallis and then under his interim replacement, knew how stubborn the neutrals could be. He and the Acadians loathed each other. Lawrence wrote to London complaining about their "treachery" and "obstinacy," and he called their neutral position "affected." Why, these Acadians were downright ungrateful to the English who had been so lenient towards them! He was convinced he could get them to finally swear an oath rather than risk choosing a side or go into self-exile.

Lawrence's subordinate officers considered him dictatorial, and he had all the diplomacy skills of a cannon, but his goal at this point may have been plain submission, not getting rid of the neutrals altogether. But for him, it would have been a short leap.

By 1755, the French and English were back to fighting in the American colonies—again, both sides forgetting to say, oh, by the way, we're at war. Since the English planned to attack Beauséjour in New Brunswick, Lawrence had canoes and boats impounded that might smuggle supplies to the French, and he ordered the Acadians to surrender their guns. The Acadians complained they needed their boats to fish and their guns to protect their livestock from wild animals. A petition complained to Lawrence, "We are grieved, Sir, at seeing ourselves declared guilty without being aware of having disobeyed."

When the Acadian representatives came to Halifax and got their chance to meet with Lawrence and his council of advisers, he launched into a vicious diatribe, accusing them of providing aid to the enemy and overcharging the British for supplies. If they swore a loyalty oath on the spot, they might redeem themselves.

The Acadians must have stared at each other over this sudden demand, and they asked if they could go home and consult their communities. The answer was a stern no—it didn't matter what the communities thought, they could swear for themselves. The Acadians still balked. They asked to consider the issue, went outside the meeting room and came back an hour later offering to swear an oath that didn't obligate them to fight—in other words, the kind of oath they had agreed to more than 30 years ago.

Not good enough, they were told. You'll take the same oath as any other British subject.

These men were put in an impossible situation, speaking for a population of what was by then 12,000 settlers. If they took the oath and France ever won the upper hand in Nova Scotia, their people were bound to face harsh reprisals. They also didn't fancy risking their lives and land fighting for the English. When the Acadians brought back their next answer, it was still no. But they didn't realize—indeed they couldn't know at all—that

Lawrence and his council had decided this was *it*. They would never get the chance to modify their view.

The word from London had been for Lawrence to "use the greatest caution and prudence in (his) conduct towards these neutrals." His orders were even to assure them they could stay "under proper regulations." Lawrence, however, decided to overstep his authority and impose his own solution to the problem. The Acadian representatives were told they would be treated as subjects of France and then tossed onto George Island, which the English used as a prison for thieves and pirates. Thousands of neutrals who had lived more than 40 years under British rule were to be deported out of Nova Scotia. Acadians would call it *Le Grand Dérangement*.

In the hot August of 1755, British soldiers began rounding them up, separating them from their homes and livestock, commanding them to take only a small quantity of possessions. Lawrence ordered his men to "destroy all the villages" and "to use every other method of distress" to find those who had escaped into the forests. By mid-September, with delays in ship charters and poor weather slowing the progress of the expulsion, Lawrence wrote to Lieutenant-Colonel Robert Mockton, "I would have you not wait for the Wives & Children coming in but ship off the men without them."

Lawrence didn't care whether the holds of the ships were overcrowded with locked up deportees, and that only a few prisoners were ever allowed up on deck to breathe fresh air—better to ensure they couldn't make trouble. The Acadians were dispersed over several of the American colonies, taken to places where they faced hostile English settlers. Some were dumped as far away as the Falkland Islands.

In that same September 1755, *The Pennsylvania Gazette* called the expulsion "a great and noble scheme."

In all, 10,000 Acadians were sent into exile, with 7000 that year alone. One third of them never survived to struggle for life in new locales, dying of smallpox and other diseases. The expulsion continued relentlessly over the next eight years. Those who fought back were to be hunted down, while others managed to escape—sometimes with the help of Mi'kmaq allies—to Québec. They tried to settle in France, but it never welcomed the exiles and treated them like a problem to be quickly dispensed with. Then enthusiasm grew for a new home: Louisiana. Contrary to myth, the Acadians were never deported there. It was a refuge they sought for themselves.

In 1760, Charles Lawrence, after suffering a high fever, died suddenly at the age of 59. His tomb lies in the basement of St. Paul's Church in downtown Halifax. Hardly anyone comes to see it.

The Expulsion of the Acadians is a dark chapter in how the English created Canada—"create" is a word we perhaps shouldn't use, since they came close to destroying a unique element of culture that we now hold dear. The best answer to the ruthless strategies of inhuman extermination is always simple for a people: *endure*. The Acadians have. Their culture remains a minority within New Brunswick and Nova Scotia, but it's still alive.

Knowledge of this episode of ethnic cleansing in Canada seems to be pitifully limited. In 2001, Bloc Québecois MP Stéphane Bergeron, a descendant of Acadians, introduced an unusual motion in the House of Commons. He suggested Canada make a formal request of the Queen to apologize for the mass deportation and what some have called war crimes of 1755. Whether apologies for historical wrongs are useful or really worth pursuing is not an issue to be debated here—just consider that the subcommittee reviewing the motion actually asked that Bergeron and others show historical evidence! The MP was incredulous. "I even had colleagues who doubted that such an event could have taken place in Canada."

The Acadians didn't get their apology, but in 2003 Queen Elizabeth II did sign a royal proclamation drafted by the Chrétien government acknowledging "historical facts and the trials and suffering experienced by the Acadian people during the Great Upheaval." (Then the proclamation niftily adds a clause to get out of legal and financial responsibility on the part of all concerned.)

Out of the dark chapter of the Upheaval came more than destruction, of course. Cornwallis went home, Lawrence left his dark legacy, but there is still a city facing the blue of the Atlantic: beautiful Halifax.

And the English were only four years away from leaving an indelible stamp on Canada and changing the fate of the entire North American continent.

THE ENGLISH CONQUER NEW FRANCE...THEN SAVE IT

As a general rule, it's probably a good idea not to put a manic-depressive in charge of your army. Many people, from politicians to his own fellow officers, didn't think James Wolfe was up to the job of taking Québec. Just going by appearances alone, Wolfe was a strange character, tall and gangly with a long nose and red hair. He had plenty to be depressed about, suffering from a slew of health problems—kidney stones, rheumatism, even bad seasickness when he had to cross the Atlantic. He lacked charm and didn't know how to talk to women, though he eventually got himself a fiancée. As for the manic side of the equation, he certainly had his moments.

One night before heading back to Canada, for instance, he was invited to dinner at the house of the de facto prime minister, William Pitt (known as Pitt the Elder, since his son would be called William as well). Pitt was

Wolfe's ultimate boss, so a little tact and decorum were in order. But Wolfe got up from the table, took out his sword and began slashing it around and playing with it while making all sorts of bizarre threats and boasts.

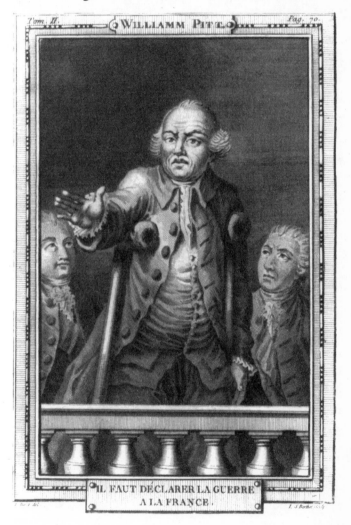

William Pitt, depicted on crutches because of his severe gout, urges Parliament to fight France in the New World.

Another guest was sure Wolfe couldn't be drunk, since he hadn't had much wine. After Wolfe left, Pitt looked to others in dismay and commented, "To think that I have committed the fate of my country and of my ministry into such hands."

Pitt was one to talk. There were many who doubted his sanity over the years, with even the young George III later calling him mad.

By the time their work was done, Wolfe would be dead (he expected to die young, and it was probably his best career move) and Pitt was out of the government. That brings us to another unusual facet of Canadian history. The aftermath of the Battle of the Plains of Abraham was as crucial to how the English created Canada as was the battle itself. Ironically, the English defeated the French, then turned around and provided survival mechanisms for them in Québec that ensured they were a lasting presence in North America.

First we have to explain the Seven Years' War. With luck, it won't take seven years to understand it. It was really two different struggles, one on each hemisphere. In Europe, Frederick the Great of Prussia was having himself a fine old time as a closet bisexual, a patron of the arts and a pal of French writer Voltaire (he wanted to be more than pals; Voltaire didn't). Surrounded by forces that were less than sociable, Frederick decided to invade Saxony. Britain, which had recently allied itself with Frederick to protect the tiny German state of Hanover, took his side. The most recent British rulers were, after all, German imports. George I couldn't speak a word of English when he sat on the throne, and his son, George II, was born nowhere near the British Isles—he came into the world right in Dad's good old, familiar Hanover. To this day, you'll run into reporters, "journos," in London who refer to Elizabeth II and her family as "The Germans." The snide remark isn't far off.

One of Frederick's newest foes was Austria, which turned to one of its own newest allies, France. Russia would also get into the act. Frederick had his highs and lows—there were amazing, exciting battles, but…that's as much as you really need to know here about the Seven Years' War in Europe, unless you want to sleep through Stanley Kubrick's interminably dull film involving the conflict, *Barry Lyndon*.

By now, you're asking—and you should be asking—how does this possibly relate back to Canada? If George II had got his way, it probably wouldn't. He was pushing for the British army to keep on helping Frederick, which would mean helping Hanover. But William Pitt—who didn't like the king very much and hardly liked anyone else—had different ideas. Pitt thought Frederick was a brilliant strategist who could manage well enough on the continent, and he also decided it was more convenient to pay him subsidies to fight the war than to sacrifice British soldiers. Pitt had plans for those men elsewhere.

You can appreciate his logic. What did the country stand to gain from its investment of men and materials to fight for Prussia? The protection of tiny little Hanover? What good was *that* to England? Across the sea, the English had already colonized large chunks of North America while the French hadn't kept up their population numbers in New France.

Historians have called William Pitt everything from the "marvel of the century" to the "perfect Machiavellian." Plagued by gout for much of his life, he seemed to have a tireless energy nonetheless, and like Wolfe, he suffered bouts of depression. From all accounts, he was an incredible ham in Parliament, complete with over-theatrical gestures, but he was considered eloquent and could pack them in. Those who ruled never liked him, but they did respect him and knew they had to use him.

At the time, the man who made the big decisions in British government policy was the Duke of Newcastle, a hollow, power-hungry creature whom writer Horace Walpole described as having "the perpetual air of a solicitor." It was Newcastle who brought Pitt into government, and you can tell how much North America meant to Newcastle through a quick anecdote. A general recommended that Annapolis be defended, and he declared, "Oh, yes, Annapolis must be defended, Annapolis should be defended." Then with unintentional but perfect comedic timing, Newcastle asked, "Where is Annapolis?"

Pitt would know. North America, specifically Canada, was where his new dream of an empire would become real, would take root. Instead of fighting Russians or Austrians, Pitt wanted Englishmen to go after the French, whom he hated, and when that was done, he thought they ought to go after the Spanish. And Pitt was certain he was indispensable. "I know that I can save this country, and that no one else can," he declared. Modesty wasn't one of his failings. Thanks to a brief military career, he assumed he understood enough to micromanage the theatre of war in Canada.

For a while, there was nothing terribly decisive in how the British and French handled the campaign over here. The French took Fort Oswego on Lake Ontario and Fort William Henry on Lake Champlain. But the French had their problems. For one thing, the governor of New France was the Marquis de Vaudreuil. And the general sent from the old country to help him—*the* general who took those important forts—was Louis-Joseph, the Marquis de Montcalm. They detested each other.

Vaudreuil was 60, born to privilege in Québec and happy to let his finance minister, François Bigot, steal the colony blind. Complaining over how Bigot diverted subsidies intended for the natives, Montcalm wrote, "If the savages had actually received a quarter of what has been allocated to them, the King would have every last red man on his side, and the English would have none."

Montcalm and Vaudreuil were different ages, had different outlooks on the world and saw things differently on matters both crucial and trivial. Vaudreuil was a commander-in-chief of the army who could appreciate the Canadien militia and their adaptation to fighting Indian style with sniper tactics. Montcalm favoured traditional warfare, and he had the record to show his methods worked. At 47, he had been trained in military discipline since he was a boy of nine; he was a career soldier who resented how the Québec colonists treated his troops like invaders instead of their rescue party. He also knew the British had no such division in their ranks, and by the start of 1759, he expected his side to lose. "Unless we have unexpected luck, or stage a diversion elsewhere in North America, or the British commit egregious military errors, Canada will fall during the coming campaign season."

Louisbourg was the first key, and the British sent over a fleet of 39 ships with 2000 mounted guns to blow the living daylights out of the French stronghold on the Nova Scotia coast. During the siege that lasted two months, even the wife of the French governor was firing cannons back at the British. Pitt had directly ordered Louisbourg to be "totally demolished." Thirty-one-year-old brigadier general James Wolfe was among the first to invade at a treacherous coastal spot at Ile Royale (another

20 grenadiers drowned when their boat was wrecked trying to reach the location).

When the news of Louisbourg's fall finally got back to London, an overjoyed Pitt grabbed and hugged the officer who informed him. Wolfe, on his return to England, began badgering Pitt with letters, asking for a new assignment. His first choice was to go to Germany, where he could fight for a general he admired, Frederick the Great. But he would settle for being part of Pitt's grand plan to invade Québec. It was only weeks later, after Wolfe's sword antics at dinner, that Pitt had his doubts about the young man he'd put in charge of capturing his new English empire. News of Wolfe's questionable mental state reached George II, who thought this was just great. "Mad is he? Then I hope he will bite some of my generals."

The French were well aware the British had their sights on Québec. When you break down the numbers, you can see they were in big trouble. Twenty-nine ships (onboard one was the future explorer James Cook) were coming with thousands of troops, 40,000 cannonballs, surgeons, even children and livestock animals. Wolfe's force was bigger than the entire colonial population of Québec! The fact that this armada could come at all meant Britain had little to worry about at sea and it could interfere with the French supply line. Wolfe, who had fought in the terrible Battle of Culloden, had recruited Scottish Highlanders as mercenaries, knowing they were fierce fighters. If Scottish Canadians take any pride in their ancestors fighting at Québec, their enthusiasm might be dampened by the fact that Wolfe said it would be "no great mischief" if these men were killed.

When he reached Beaumont on the St. Lawrence River, Wolfe arranged to have a piece of propaganda nailed onto a church door, one he had personally written. His forces, he explained, were "to check the insolence of France," and he wanted the Canadiens to know that George II had no quarrel with the "industrious peasant" of New France. With all the tension and distrust between the French army and the Canadiens at this time, this tactic might have been effective—if only Wolfe hadn't promised to show them no mercy and ruthlessly destroy their land and homes if they fought.

But Wolfe had a surprise coming to him when his fleet sailed into the St. Lawrence up to what is now Québec City and he finally got a look at the fortress he was supposed to take. There it was, 90 metres above the river basin behind its walls, overlooking the Lower Town and the suburbs of St.-Roch and Palais. Montcalm, not being a fool, had fortified the nearby banks of the river and surrounding hills. He deployed Canadien militia upriver and had his second-in-command, Louis Antoine de Bougainville, commanding a mobile force of about 1000 men in case Wolfe tried to land above his target. Montcalm clearly still didn't have much faith in holding out; he kept his supply ships 80 kilometres up the St. Lawrence, just in case he needed to quit Québec altogether.

Montcalm sent fire-rafts toward Wolfe's anchored ships. Wolfe got so sick of this tactic he sent Montcalm a personal letter telling him to knock it off. He threatened to lash the fire-rafts to the ships carrying Canadien prisoners. Within a few days, Wolfe was blasting away at Québec's walls, relying on the same siege warfare that had crushed Louisbourg. In one evening, 50 of the Lower Town's houses were destroyed. By mid-August, more than half the town was rubble.

But Wolfe was frustrated. As long as Montcalm stayed behind Québec's walls, the English general was running out of time as much as his French enemy. When the St. Lawrence iced over, he would be stuck. His own brigadiers, all aristocrats from better families who could look down on the young commander, were starting to doubt he could handle the job. Two of these were men he knew well, Robert Monckton and James Murray. The third was George Townshend, an ambitious MP who had served at Culloden but who had never had a proper command before and who lobbied Pitt to get his post. Townshend complained in letters about Wolfe's judgment. He was skilled at drawing snide cartoon caricatures, and he made his commander one of his subjects.

Wolfe lost his patience. He sent orders, countermanded them, sent new ones, all in less than a day. Without bothering to consult his brigadiers, he launched an invasion of 4000 men upriver at Beauport, where Montcalm's army in force must have thought they were having a turkey shoot. Wolfe's soldiers couldn't even return fire, and he suffered 440 casualties. Wolfe now resorted to pillaging the countryside and burning towns, something he had already promised in correspondence—that he would "leave famine and desolation behind me."

Not that it broke the stalemate. Both commanders were getting worn down. Wolfe was sick with fever and enduring the agony of kidney stones, taking opiates and that cure-all of 18th-century medicine: regular bleedings. Montcalm was in better physical shape, but just as emotionally miserable. He had received news that one of his daughters was dead, and he missed his wife back home in France.

Desperate, Wolfe finally left his sickbed to inspect the north shore and came up with an insane idea. Of course, insane ideas sometimes work. He also may have been inspired by information from a former British prisoner of war, Robert Stobo, who apparently once drew a sketch of the defences of Fort Duquesne (Pittsburgh)—and was stupid enough to sign it—right before he was found guilty of being a spy and transferred to Québec. Instead of making his assault far up the river at Cap Rouge, Wolfe had decided to land his men at Anse au Foulon, a few kilometres west of Québec, and have them scale the cliffs to the Plains of Abraham (a name that sounds Biblical, but actually comes from the first name of a Scot farmer).

He still hadn't told his brigadiers his plan, and they finally sent him a letter on the fleet's flagship asking, in effect, "Umm, hey, Boss, you want to clue us in on the big idea? We're only your top officers." By then, Wolfe had changed into a bright new uniform and had entrusted

"The taking of Quebeck by the English forces commanded by Gen. Wolfe, Sep: 13th, 1759." — from London Magazine, vol. 29, June 1760

his will, his personal papers and a miniature portrait of his fiancée to a friend and naval officer. He expected his death wish to at last be fulfilled.

The St. Lawrence, like the English Thames, is a tidal river, and the oarsmen pulling the boats full of troops were fighting wind and choppy waters, trying to find their disembarking point in the dark. When a French sentry challenged the boats passing under the guns, a quick-thinking officer answered back in French. As dawn rose, a French artillery battery upriver sighted the British boats and soldiers and opened fire. Incredibly, Wolfe sent word at one point to *stop* the landings. More incredibly still, the officer ignored the order. More men hurried up the cliffs while the British light infantry fought back the French gunners.

Historians and military experts are still arguing whether Wolfe was a genius or just had plain dumb luck. Now that he was on the Plains, he could have told his men to take the highest ground, which would have helped his siege guns blow more holes in the fortress of Québec. He didn't. Of course, to be fair, that also would have put *them* in range of Québec's cannons. In hauling men, weapons and packs all the way upriver and then up the bluffs, he also didn't give himself a means of escape. As a light rain came down, he ordered his men to set up two lines and each man to load a couple of musket balls into their guns for maximum effect.

Montcalm had spent a restless night in Beauport, expecting Wolfe's attack to come there. When a man escaping the sentry skirmish raced up, panting and frantically warning that the Brits were at the bluffs, no one believed him. No one even bothered to wake Montcalm up to tell him. Eventually, enough warnings came in that the general was roused from his bed, and he sent word for four regular battalions to be deployed at Québec's walls. He was riding on the road from his house when he ran into the last person he wanted to meet (except, of course, the enemy): Vaudreuil. The governor of New France still angrily insisted the attack was coming at Beauport.

When Montcalm finally crossed a pontoon bridge over the St. Charles River and saw what was waiting for him on the Plains, he was in shock. "They are not where they are supposed to be!" he said.

Montcalm had sent an urgent message to Bougainville's mobile force at Cap Rouge, but he decided not to wait. He thought he better attack sooner than later because the enemy was probably entrenching. Actually, Wolfe wasn't. He hadn't even ordered entrenching tools to be hauled out from the ships. The French gunners were sending cannonballs at the British, and Wolfe had told them to lie down while light infantrymen dealt with Native and Canadien snipers. If Montcalm had been patient, Bougainville could have attacked Wolfe from the west, and we might all be speaking French today.

Riding along his line of troops, Montcalm thought a little pep talk was in order. "Are you tired?" he asked the men. "No!" they shouted back, which sounded all well and good but probably wasn't accurate. At ten o'clock, knowing the British troops were better trained and having his own doubts in the Canadien militia, Montcalm sent his forces out in a frontal assault.

In Canada, we've been infected to some degree by American myths, and one is that the redcoats must have been idiots to stand in the open and fire while clever and plucky revolutionaries shot guerrilla warfare-style on the ground. You get this everywhere, from idle chatter to Disney's film version of *Johnny Tremain*. It makes one wonder how the British army could win if the French had not only their own troops but also the Canadien militia and Natives who fought like the Iroquois?

It was never that simple. From an ordinary private's perspective in 1759, warfare was a terrifying situation on the gut level. You were supposed to *stand there*, fire your musket, stand or kneel to load for a second volley—and hope like hell the enemy didn't blow you to pieces with its own musket fire or a cannonball that could cut you in two. And if you got through that, well, great, lucky you—now the white-coated French soldiers were running *at you* as you fixed your bayonet and rushed forward, shouting, about to kill the guy who decided that you'd do as his personal practice dummy. Worse, surgeons were still appallingly ignorant of anatomical details, let alone the causes of disease and infection, so you could die of even superficial wounds.

You won battles like this with timed volleys and carefully choreographed manoeuvres, and through the discipline of facing down both the psychological threat and the very tangible artillery barrage. Wolfe's men were seasoned fighters, and even if they broke, there was no place to run. When Montcalm's men rushed forward to about 150 yards of the British line to fire, they didn't shirk. The British soldiers who were hit fell and the ranks closed up. Wolfe's men still didn't fire back yet.

This is where the second big failing happened on the French side. Montcalm's professional soldiers stopped to reload, standing as usual. The Canadien militia dropped to the ground or took cover to reload, relying on *their* usual method. The Canadiens advanced and fired all out of step, so that there was no real impact on the enemy line. The British waited for them to get closer and began to mow them down. The effect was devastating.

As the musket smoke cleared, the Canadiens had the terrifying view of British soldiers already reloaded, about to fire again.

Then, as the English plodded forward with their bayonets, the Highlanders, led by James Murray, gave chase with their Claymores (*Claymore* is Gaelic for "great sword"; it should actually be Gaelic for "great, *big, honking* sword" since one of these weapons weighs more than two kilograms and would be ideal if you wanted to filet the enemy). The Scots put on a fierce show, but the rain was gone, the sun breaking through, and they got the worst of the bloody fighting near the woods on the northern edge of the plains. On the right, the Louisbourg Grenadiers were taking losses from snipers in a cornfield.

Wolfe had been wounded early in the fighting, since he was in range for the militiamen in the bushes above the St. Lawrence. He was shot through the right wrist, and he wrapped it up in a handkerchief. Then he was shot again, this time in the groin. Finally, two shots hit him in the chest, the final fatal wounds. In his last moments, Wolfe—who's been called a neurotic hypochondriac—wasn't thinking about his ailments but waving his hat to signal a manoeuvre for one of the units. A couple of men moved him a few hundred yards away from the fighting, and he asked them to set him down. He was hemorrhaging and he knew he wouldn't last long. He told those nearby to forget about getting the surgeon. One man watching the fleeing French said, "They run, see how they run."

"Who runs?" asked Wolfe, who must have already been slipping into shock.

"The enemy, sir," replied the officer. "Egad, they give way everywhere."

At this, Wolfe supposedly gave some final orders and said before dying, "Now, God be praised, I will die in peace." We'll never be sure what he actually said, because versions differ. An officer cynically noted "many, from a vanity of talking, claimed the honour of being his supporters, after he was wounded."

With Wolfe gone, command fell to Monckton—who had it for all of a few minutes. He was shot in the lungs and was carried away to one of the ships. George Townshend was now in charge simply because he was the one brigadier the men could track down. Fortunately, he realized that the perfect discipline of the British was starting to unravel, and he sent orders to the battalion commanders to regroup. Bougainville's mobile force had finally arrived from Cap Rouge, but shocked at what he saw, he pulled his men off to a nearby wood.

Montcalm, meanwhile, was dying. During the retreat, he had been hit in the chest and the leg with grapeshot, but had bravely struggled to keep order, sending advice to Vaudreuil and dictating a letter for Townshend. For the sake of his men, he asked his enemy, "Do not let them perceive that they have changed masters. Be their protector as I have been their father." He died early the next morning.

It was over, a battle that lasted mere minutes. When the British heard their general was dead, many broke into tears. It would take a long time for news of the victory to cross the Atlantic, but when it did, it prompted huge celebrations in England. By the end of October, there were already two books rushed into print to satisfy reader interest in the battle details.

If the story were being told in one of those 1930s black and white British historical dramas (maybe with the delicately featured Leslie Howard playing Wolfe), the letters for *The End* would come up superimposed over a bell tolling the victory. Fade to black. Wolfe's last words, true or not, certainly wrap it up nicely in Hollywood fashion. But that wasn't the end, not even close, and what happened after the battle would change the whole continent.

The British had suffered 58 killed and about 600 wounded, which was almost exactly the same casualty list as the French. And they were also still outside Québec's walls.

Vaudreuil, who made sure he blamed the defeat on Montcalm in the future to avoid winding up in the Bastille, ordered a panicked retreat from Beauport, leaving behind a lot of ammunition and provisions. Bougainville's force was used to defend the rear, and Vaudreuil left more than 2000 men, mostly Canadien militia, to literally hold the fort. The British consolidated their position over the next three days, and just when they were ready to hammer Québec's walls again, the French ordered a cease-fire to their guns and sent out a flag of truce. The Union Jack was raised near the top of Mountain Street on September 18.

The British terms were generous. They had to be, because both sides were exhausted, crops were bad, winter was coming, and the British still weren't in a position where they could control the French colony. Instead of becoming prisoners of war, French army regulars were transported home under a flag of truce. Militiamen could stay with their families if they were willing to swear a loyalty oath. And most importantly, they could keep practicing their Catholic faith. These terms would be close to the ones for the formal capitulation of New France negotiated later by Vaudreuil. Townshend went back to England, while James Murray was stuck with the unenviable task of holding onto Québec.

And the French weren't quite ready to let go of it yet. François-Gaston de Lévis, once Montcalm's second-in-command, was now his replacement. Lévis came up in the spring with men who had survived the harsh winter in Montréal, which had enjoyed a much better crop harvest than Québec. He didn't have the guns for a long siege, but with luck, reinforcements would come from France before the British fleet returned.

Historians like to write that Murray lacked judgment or was reckless in his next action. Let's call it what it was: a really bone-headed move. If anything, Murray should have known not to come out from behind the walls of Québec and commit the very same error that Montcalm had made. But since he thought, "our little Army was in the habit of beating that Enemy," he pitted the seasoned British troops against the French militia in a replay of last year's battle. His men found themselves leg-deep in melting snow while their 20 pieces of field artillery got stuck in the mud. When it was over, the British lost 259 men, far more than in the first battle. The only saving grace was that after the British retreat, the French didn't recapture Québec. By mid-July, the British fleet was back, making it clear to the French more than anything else that the cause was lost.

You would think Pitt was happy. Oh, but he wasn't. Peace talks dragged over the years of 1761 and 1762, with France trying to bargain away Canada in exchange for recovering the captured West Indies island of Guadeloupe, which had the lucrative sugar trade. Pitt wouldn't budge, and by the time negotiations for the Treaty of Paris were reopened he was out of the picture. He was pushing for England to go after his next target, Spain, but no one would support a long war getting bigger, and a war with new combatants. When Pitt finally caved and quit the Cabinet, he broke down and wept in front of the king.

Back in Québec, James Murray became the first British governor for 65,000 French Catholics. He preferred them to the Protestant English merchants who were eager to sail over and cash in on Britain's latest conquest, calling them "the most immoral collection of men I ever knew." A lousy general, Murray was a competent administrator who protected the right of the French to worship as they pleased and to sit on juries (he was less enlightened toward other peoples, keeping and later selling a young black female slave). His successor and fellow veteran of the battle on the Plains of Abraham, Guy Carleton, would see things the same way, wanting to leave the French be and without the yoke of English law.

We shouldn't overstate the case. Murray and Carleton were there at ground zero with thousands of French, and they both were probably more motivated by enlightened self-interest than enlightened tolerance. Murray made his argument with numbers. Carleton talked about harmony. Murray was a Scot and Carleton was Irish; while loyal British officers, they had some idea of the friction English law could cause with defeated though still proud populations, laws that were dictated from an England thousands of kilometres away.

Ultimately, the survival and perseverance of the Québecois was an accomplishment of a unique people itself. But whatever the motives of the British officers, their actions inadvertently helped save them. The Acadians had almost been wiped off the Canadian map altogether; the Québecois were not. Murray's efforts, and as we'll see, Carleton's initiatives later, also helped hold back a slower, silent death of assimilation. There was even more cultural fallout from the battle to come.

As time passed, Wolfe's stature only grew—much to the bitter resentment of James Murray. He had to live the rest of his days with the embarrassment that he nearly undid everything gained by Wolfe in his battle against Lévis. For years, Murray hoped certain truths (that is, ones that helped his reputation) would "come out by degrees" about the Québec campaign. They never did. Wolfe's memory had its protectors, including his caricaturist George Townshend, who didn't want to see any book or article have "disagreeable consequence." Ever the political weasel, Townshend sent his correspondence with Murray off to Sir Jeffrey Amherst, who had become Britain's commander-in-chief of the army.

The last thing Amherst needed by then was Wolfe's legend being called into question, especially with American colonists to the south starting to grumble about paying more taxes to have a large British army sticking around to protect them.

The Wolfe legend was firmly in place years later, with the dead hero getting a memorial in Westminster Abbey and a statue in Greenwich. It got another big boost when Pennsylvania artist Benjamin West chose him as a subject. West didn't care about the battle details for his grand painting of *The Death of General Wolfe*, insisting, "Wolfe must not die like a common soldier under a bush." Instead, Wolfe dies in a Christ-like pose with a Native man crouched down in the posture of a "noble savage"—which is odd, because any Natives on the scene were fighting for the French. And as historians have pointed out, some of the "apostles" surrounding the dying hero weren't even in Québec when Wolfe died.

The Death of General Wolfe, by Benjamin West

It didn't matter. The painting was a success, with long queues for the viewing in 1771 outside the Royal Academy, an organization Benjamin West later ran as its president.

Of course, every hardworking creative type knows deep down there's a little (or a large) hack inside, and West could tell he was onto something good—so he churned out five more versions, including one for the family of Robert Monckton. Like the Native man painted in, you'll recall Monckton wasn't there to see Wolfe die either, but he got place of honour in the composition just the same, crouching down near the dying hero. This copy is the one that hangs today in the Sigmund Samuel Gallery of the Royal Ontario Museum.

Thousands of ordinary folks in London couldn't afford to buy a canvas like George III or Monckton's family, so they settled for a cheaper, immensely popular engraving by William Wollett. Wolfe was a kind of British

James Dean, the warrior-hero dying young and pre-served in the pop art of his time.

West always hoped one day to get another big smash, hoping he wasn't a one-hit wonder. In 1802, he got to have dinner with Horatio Nelson, who had been born a year before the battle on the Plains of Abraham and was in awe of Wolfe's accomplishments. "I never pass a print-shop, where your *Death of General Wolfe* is in the window, without being stopped by it," he told the artist.

West must have smiled at this wonderful compliment, and it sparked a perverse invitation. He wanted to do another canvas on a similar idea to his masterpiece, but he didn't have a worthy enough subject—maybe the naval hero could inspire "another such scene"? Instead of taking offence, Nelson warmed to the idea. "Then I hope I shall die in the next battle!"

It took three years and wasn't the next battle, but Nelson eventually got his wish. And West painted Nelson dying nobly on his ship, *Victory*, with the same motif of a griev-ing crowd. If you ever get to see the work, it's stiff and calculated. *The Death of General Wolfe* is by far a superior painting. No problem—in time, the naval hero got an entire tourist site in the form of Trafalgar Square and his own memorial column.

We keep the heroes who prove durable. Nelson the admiral was always more relevant to the English, while Wolfe's accomplishment was a distant affair. Though English, he could be adopted by Canadians.

His durability, or lack thereof, says a lot about who we are now. In the year of Confederation, a Scottish immi-grant schoolteacher and Orangeman, Alexander Muir, saddled us with a hymn almost as jingoistic as the "rockets' red glare" of our southern cousins. *The Maple Leaf Forever*—which has an annoying tune far harder to carry than *O Canada*—mercifully died out in popularity by the time Québec was talking separatism in the 1960s, sparing thousands of schoolchildren from having to learn it. This is its original first verse:

> *Wolfe the dauntless hero came,*
> *And planted firm Britannia's flag,*
> *On Canada's fair domain*

No one sings it much anymore—certainly not with the original words. (CBC's *Metro Morning* show in Toronto ran a contest in 1997 for new words, and the winner was a Romanian immigrant whose revamped lyrics read like a cross between a travel show jingle and grade school poetry.)

A song is one thing. English Canada found more permanent ways to rub Québec's nose in the victory of the Plains of Abraham. Right outside the *Musée national des beaux-arts du Québec* still stands a commemorative column that can remind any Québecois what was lost. An inscription on the obelisk used to read: HERE DIED WOLFE VICTORIOUS. The memorial kept getting defaced, and the FLQ chose it as a bomb target in the '60s. Finally, it was decided a neutral tone was in order, so the obelisk now simply reads: HERE DIED WOLFE.

As this book was being edited, the National Battlefields Commission of the federal government was busy organizing a re-enactment of the battle for the 250th anniversary. It wouldn't be the first time it's held a replay of Wolfe against Montcalm, and when it had spectators a decade ago, the government decided the battle would go over better if it was declared "a draw." What could be more thoroughly Canadian?

But after Quebec sovereigntists protested and called a celebration and re-enactment for 2009 offensive and insulting, the Commission—as we go to press—has decided to call it off. Because of "excessive language and threats," the chairman has said it can't ensure the safety of the public. The groups who hated the planned events have declared victory. The NDP's deputy leader has argued it was wrong to call off the celebration out of fear—but then he thought it was wrong to put it on in the first place (so he gets to have it both ways). And what seems to be forgotten is an important point. The Commission didn't concede sovereigntists were right on the merits of their arguments; it all but confessed it had been intimidated by a bogeyman of past separatist violence. This controversy, too, as we'll find out, is thoroughly Canadian, and as we explore how the English created Canada, we will find ourselves coming full circle: back to the Plains, back to what the English did and didn't do and how violence on battlefields and in the streets have shaped the nation we are today.

THE RIPPLES THAT STILL FLOW

B ritain no longer had to worry about France in North America. But it was the French who made bargains with various Native peoples and who struck alliances and intermarried with the women of different tribes. Now the French were subdued and there was a new superpower on the continent, one that couldn't be trusted. In 1763, a war chief of the Ottawa, Pontiac, decided the British had to be driven out.

Both American and Canadian historians have taken to casually referring to this as a Native *rebellion*, but the word "rebellion" implies the Native peoples were conquered or owed allegiance already to the British forces. This certainly was not the case. Pontiac and those who supported his cause wanted to ensure they weren't driven out, assimilated or outright exterminated. An Ojibwa chief told English traders bluntly, "We are not your slaves. These lakes, these woods and mountains were left to us by our ancestors…"

For a while, the war tribes captured fort after fort in the American colonies. It was common for Natives to strip captured prisoners, cut off their hands and feet, burn them alive and practice more gruesome tortures. The attacks spread terror, but they failed to drive out the British as Pontiac hoped. He never managed to stir the Natives' old allies, the French Canadians, to open rebellion or to provide much help, and the politics and alliances of the various tribes involved were complex. At the height of an assault on Fort Detroit, his own men abandoned the fight to go home for the hunting season.

Pontiac's own people, the Ottawa, turned on him after a peace deal was finally worked out with the English. Young men bullied him to the point where he fled with his family to the safety of in-laws in Illinois. In April 1769, a Peoria warrior clubbed him and stabbed him to death at a trading post near St. Louis.

What came out of this bloody conflict was a curious English document, which is usually referred to simply as the Royal Proclamation of 1763. It still has ramifications for how Canada deals with aboriginal peoples.

It was the conception of the Secretary of State responsible for the colonies, George Montagu-Dunk, the second Earl of Halifax (and the man whom the capital of Nova Scotia is named after). The document was essentially designed to assure the Natives that Britain had no imperial ambitions for their land. It was rushed through Cabinet, got the equivalent of a rubber stamp from the Privy Council and then was promulgated by George III.

In its wording, the Royal Proclamation of 1763 was supposed to help define the colonies (Cape Breton, for instance, was now to go to Nova Scotia), but more importantly, it set down some rules for dealings with Native peoples, reserving, for instance, "for the use of the...Indians, all the Lands and Territories not included within (our) Limits or within the Limits of the Territory granted to the Hudson's Bay Company." *No one*—no surveyor or colonial government—could go ahead and operate, trade or settle this land without the Crown's authority or through its representatives. If that sounds like the waters got even muddier over the Native peoples' rights to the land and the Crown's usage, you're absolutely right. But at least it pushed out third parties and tried to keep the squabble, at least on paper, between the Crown and aboriginal peoples.

So this is the mother of all documents, really, when it comes down to aboriginal land claims in Canada. And its legacy is still very much with us. In the Canadian Charter of Rights and Freedoms, Section 25 makes it clear that the Earl of Halifax's document is still binding. It "shall not be construed so as to abrogate or derogate... any rights or freedoms that have been recognized by the Royal Proclamation of October 7, 1763." When the English helped create Canada, they had no idea they were helping to create it for more than just the English and French Canadians.

Historians suggest Halifax always meant it to be the start of the process, not an end in itself. The wording was vague on many points and created whole new head-aches—not the least of which for Québec. Under the proclamation, the newly defined colonies were supposed to run "agreeable to the laws of England." Oh, really? So much then for the Treaty of Paris, which in plain black ink made it clear that Canadiens could stay Catholic and were allowed to hold government offices (something Catholics couldn't do back in England at the time).

To the rescue came Sir Guy Carleton, who apparently recognized the contradiction for Québec early on. Carleton is a fascinating, enigmatic character. He was an early advocate of Québecois rights, opposing British merchant complaints over Canadien manufacturing and taking steps to protect the French claim to a winter seal fishery off the St. Lawrence. At the time, his job wasn't paid through a salary but through fees charged for every service. Carleton decided he wouldn't accept any.

As far as he was concerned, his predecessor in governing Québec, James Murray, went too far in exerting Britain's will. The key to Québec, thought Carleton, was to reform and mould the French laws, not replace them with English ones. For Carleton, "the British form of government, transplanted into this continent, never will produce the same fruits as at home."

In 1770, Carleton was back in London pushing for his vision of a Québec under French civil law. It took four years, but he got it. Under the Québec Act, Catholics could legally practice their religion and were allowed to hold public office, while land ownership followed the old system that went back to the age of Cardinal Richelieu.

By now you might want to remind me that this book is titled *How the English Created Canada*, not "how it created Québec." But this new legislation was also a big can of gasoline, spilling right down into a fire of growing discontent. Those in Massachusetts and Virginia called it one of "The Intolerable Acts." Of course, these Anglo-Americans were far more livid over paying higher taxes imposed from London, but this new Act, which protected a bunch of French-speaking Papists who had posed such a grim threat for so long to their upstanding American colonies...well! The timing couldn't be worse.

Soon-to-be-famous revolutionairies like Benjamin Franklin—men who would be touted as Deists and closet agnostics by so many subsequent biographers—got busy scribbling complaints about the "grave danger" posed by laws enacted hundreds of kilometres away, an obvious attack on statutes protecting the above-mentioned diabolical, threatening and oh-so-foreign Papists.

When the Americans started their revolution, they briefly got it into their heads to invade Canada. This was after their less than persuasive attempts to sway the Québecois to their cause, offering them "a chance for emerging from a humiliating subjection" under "tyrants." It's hard to find this pitch sincere after your distant neighbours have whined about what a threat you and your religion are and delighted in the deportation of thousands of fellow French.

The Americans managed to take Montréal, mostly because the city had few defences and next to no voluntary militia. They would find out soon enough that occupying the city was far harder than capturing it. Any Canadien goodwill quickly soured when the Americans banned Christmas Mass and took to arresting suspected Loyalists.

The Americans expected their whole invasion of Canada to be a cake walk...and forgot about the icing. Ignoring the fact that winter was coming, Benedict Arnold was convinced he'd make Guy Carleton surrender Québec in less than a month. Within weeks, his starving men had to eat their own shoe leather. The arrogant Arnold had never bothered to consult an accurate map—what he thought was 180 miles (290 kilometres) to Québec from Massachusetts was 350 miles (560 kilometres) that had to be crossed through snow, floods and an unforgiving wilderness.

When his wretched army, now reduced by half, finally tried to take Québec, Arnold at least got help from General Richard Montgomery's forces that were coming up from Montréal. It would not be enough. Carleton had nothing but contempt for Arnold, whom he called a "horse jockey" (the future traitor was a short fellow). He didn't have much respect for Montgomery either, and when the general sent Carleton a letter demanding surrender, Carleton's response was to burn it without even bothering to read it. Carleton, who had served as quartermaster-general under Wolfe in 1759, knew what these fortress walls could stand. He also knew where to shore up defences.

In the early morning hours of December 31, 1775, with musket fire burning through the white sheet of a full-scale blizzard, the Americans tried a two-pronged attack on Québec. Montgomery earned a bullet in the head, and his men abandoned their dead officers in the snowdrifts. Arnold, shot in the leg, was carried away from the fighting. At the end, about 400 Americans were captured with about 60 killed or wounded.

The rebel army stuck around until spring, but by May, Royal Navy ships were coming up the St. Lawrence with British reinforcements. The first invasion of Canada had been an unmitigated disaster. Back in the American colonies, a disgusted John Adams called it "half a war." This "half a war" ultimately split the province of Canada in half and divided up the colonial Maritimes.

Anglo-Americans who didn't believe in the revolutionary cause—and there were many—fled north. By 1783, there were 25,000 Loyalist refugees in Nova Scotia, half of them landing in Halifax. Tensions between the established population and the new arrivals were inevitable. Wealthier arrivals and merchants who got rich in the war bought up the best properties, setting up impressive mansions. Poor refugees quickly hauled away the discarded lumber for shacks on what is now Halifax's Market Street. Politics also divided the old settlers from the new. Loyalists just off the boat picked up a whiff of sympathy toward the rebel cause in Halifax. In the end, the British government decided it would be a good idea if there was a new separate colony. This would be New Brunswick, and it would have its own assembly.

The Loyalists who fled to Québec presented quite another problem. They found themselves under the paradox of French laws preserved by the British Crown, and they didn't like it, or their lack of representation, one bit. "We are English subjects just as they are," they complained. Meanwhile, as much as Guy Carleton had resisted giving the Québecois representative assemblies, thinking these were an English-imposed solution, the French weren't buying that argument anymore. They kept clamouring for an elected assembly as well.

Now back in London, such dilemmas could often be solved by simply drawing a new line on the map. After all, it worked for Nova Scotia and New Brunswick, didn't it? So in 1791, the Constitution Act created Upper Canada (Ontario) and Lower Canada (Québec). Even today, you run into people who use the expression "Upper Canada" or "Central Canada" (which Ontario most definitely is not, and those of us from the West know better). So now there were two Canadas. There you go—fixed.

Not quite.

A line on the map only sowed the seed for later problems. The governors for both Ontario and Québec were appointed in Britain, and these strangers sailed over and arbitrarily appointed their own councils. All these men held the power over money from Crown land reserves, and they could enact policies as they pleased and completely ignore voices of dissent in the elected assemblies. The English had failed to address the heart of the matter, and though it would take years, the cheque would come due.

Race is another legacy of the Revolutionary War.

Our country was to become a relatively safe haven for thousands of African Americans fleeing slavery, the last stop on the Underground Railroad. But how did the concept originate that *here* was a better place, that it should be a refuge? It started with the English, and unfortunately it didn't grow out of any humanitarian purpose. When the British army still had a chance of putting down the American Revolution, it was willing to take all the help it could get, including from escaped slaves. The governor of Virginia even organized an "Ethiopian Regiment," which George Washington feared could become his "most formidable enemy."

The chance granted to blacks to fight for the Loyalist cause was purely a way of exploiting the exigencies of war. The British offered freedom to any slave who escaped a rebel landowner and agreed to come over to their side—they didn't, however, make the same offer to those slaves belonging to Loyalists. Some blacks were already free citizens willing to fight. They were often skilled labourers, from blacksmiths to carpenters, and their new duties involved doing anything from cooking meals to acting as personal servants for officers. But while "Liberty to Slaves" might have been the slogan that lured them to British lines, their status remained tenuous. A servant of Guy Carleton's held a certificate of freedom; it wasn't really worth the paper it was written on, because he was regularly called the general's "property," and it was understood he couldn't leave his employer when the war was over.

Not all blacks were volunteers—many were pressed against their will into British service. And the British were quite capable of betraying those who bought into the promise of freedom for service. When the "Company of Negroes" evacuated Boston for Halifax in 1776, the idea was floated that they be ransomed back to the Americans for white Loyalist prisoners of war. Fortunately for these veterans, the suggestion wasn't adopted.

Others may have tried to do the right thing. By 1783, Guy Carleton was commander-in-chief of North America in New York, haggling with George Washington over how many blacks were "property" of American citizens and how many could evacuate to Canada after the British capitulation. Carleton stayed firm, telling Washington he would evacuate any blacks who qualified under a narrow set of terms of protection—in fact, many had been shipped out already. Washington was taken aback, but in the end he went along with it and appointed his own inspector for an examination board.

For black Loyalists, it must have been a humiliating process to have to appeal for their freedom after having already risked their lives for it through escape and military service. Ship captains faced threat of prosecution if they were discovered transporting any black who was not one of the official ones listed in Carleton's "Book of Negroes."

For those who did make it as refugees into Canada, many moving to Nova Scotia, new shocks followed. Slavery was still practiced in Canada, and black Loyalists learned they could move freely but were often treated little better than their brothers and sisters in bondage. The earliest arrivals endured winter in tents and bark shelters and waited for their meal rations on the streets. Many white Loyalists faced refugee conditions as well, but the lot for their black counterparts was worse. No white Loyalist ever faced a challenge by a visiting American who claimed they owned them—a challenge that could get legitimized by a hearing in court and that had a disturbing probability of a favourable ruling.

There were cases of enlightened kindness from the English both in Nova Scotia and from abroad. An Anglican charity group in London, which focused on the welfare of blacks in America, sent boxes of blankets, clothing and shoes in 1787 and more supplies two years later. For the most part, however, life was harsh for these new arrivals. Many blacks took jobs with pitiful wages as indentured servants. The overwhelming majority were cheated out of an inconsistent land grant system that was open to corruption and abuse.

Promises had been made. Compensation of land in Nova Scotia was supposed to be forthcoming for those who had fought for the Crown. When black Loyalists received parcels of land at all, they were modest compared to those of their white counterparts and frequently had the worst soil for growing. An official conceded later that the blacks had been victims of "an injudicious and unjust mode of assigning their lands."

Despite incredible hardships, the black Loyalists persevered. What started as a military convenience for the English became a unique voluntary migration. These arrivals fanned out across Nova Scotia, in Preston and Shelburne, in Lunenburg and St. Margaret's Bay, making them today the oldest indigenous black community in North America. That remarkable population is not in the United States, it's right here in *our* country. The Loyalists became the ancestors of what can honestly be considered—after the aboriginal nations, the English and the French—Canada's fourth founding people.

Lately, the knowledge of Canada's role in slavery—so long ignored—has been revived. Never a people to let ourselves off the hook, we now remind ourselves slavery was here, an evil practiced both under the French in Québec and under the British. There does need to be more scholarship for this period. Unfortunately, one ignorance has been exchanged for another.

The common assumption is that slavery simply ended in Canada with Britain's abolition of it in 1834. The Americans needed a war to end it for all of its states, of course, and Brazil took until 1888 before it put a stop to it. One Englishman, though, was responsible for an important milestone in Canada. And his attitudes reflected more of the growing consciousness of his home country than the conditions in Boston and Halifax.

Forget Canada and the American colonies for a moment. Attitudes toward black people in England itself were far more complex than is commonly thought today, certainly more than in the empire across the Atlantic. There were, of course, always racist idiots who compared black people to apes and those who refused to give them employment or housing. Yet marriages between black residents and the English were impressively commonplace up until around 1820. A woman of high society described the London of 1802 as having "Men of colour in the rank of gentlemen; a black lady covered with finery in the pit at the opera and tawny children playing in the squares." Bill Richmond, a former American slave, rose from working as a cabinetmaker's apprentice in York,

England, to being a famous boxer, buying a pub in London's Leicester Square and running his own fight academy.

The law was equally divided in attitudes. During the reign of Queen Anne, one chief justice declared "the law takes no notice of Negroes," while another decided, "As soon as a Negro comes to England he becomes free."

Attitudes, however, were changing. Abolitionist Granville Sharp had been fighting his cause, gathering supporters, testing the law, and by 1772, a legal case underscored the principle that slaves were free once they set foot on English soil. It was an important precedent, and now many who thought they were moral, intelligent Englishmen had to ask themselves why an evil that was banned in their home country was allowed to flourish elsewhere?

John Graves Simcoe asked himself that question.

Simcoe had navy blue in his veins, with an impressive pedigree—his father had been captain of the *Pembroke* during the siege of Louisbourg. His godfather was an admiral. That he was destined for military service isn't a big leap in imagination. But by 1775, he was already trying to raise a regiment of black Loyalists from Boston. He was 23, an age when young men—both today and then—decide on their politics but when the heart wins the argument more often than the head.

When walking the halls of Oxford or the cobbled streets of London, Simcoe in his formative early adult years would have known of Sharp's crusade. He would have been able to compare for himself free black men and women living as English equals to the wretched- ness of slaves being transported on the docks. He never got to lead a black regiment during his service in the Revolutionary War. But the cause never left him, and when he returned to become Upper Canada's governor in 1792, he famously promised he wouldn't discriminate "between the natives of Africa, America or Europe."

His possible inspiration, abolitionist pioneer Granville Sharp, was prompted to act when he came across the beaten and near-blind Jonathan Strong on the steps of a surgery in Mincing Lane in London. John Graves Simcoe was prompted to act when he heard of the case of Chloe Cooley.

The details of the case were horrific, but unfortunately, not uncommon. In 1793, slaveowner William Vrooman of Queenston had Cooley tied up with ropes and thrown into his boat, which he rowed across the Niagara River so he could sell her in New York. Cooley was screaming in protest and trying to break free. Watching all this was a free black soldier, Peter Martin, who testified to Simcoe's council meeting about the "violent outrage." Simcoe instructed the attorney general to draft a bill over slavery for when the council next met.

But slaveowners were a powerful enough group in the fledgling colony, making "arguments of the dearness of labour and the difficulty of obtaining servants to cultivate lands…." Simcoe never got slavery completely abolished, but in the political haggling that followed, he settled for killing it in slow degrees. The Act Against Slavery banned the introduction of new slaves. And the children of slaves would be freed by age 25, while any children born from them before this age were automatically free.

As Professor Afua Cooper of the University of Toronto has pointed out, this created a peculiar traffic flow. By the War of 1812, slaves from some of the United States were heading for Upper Canada in the hope of freedom, while some blacks from Upper Canada headed for spots like

Michigan and Illinois, where slavery had already been prohibited.

It was a step, a crucial step. Unfortunately, no one in the rest of British North America at the legislative level showed Simcoe's enlightened courage. One interesting strategy was for slaves in Québec to challenge their masters' legal right to hold them, and in 1797, a few won their cases. In Nova Scotia, the same method was sometimes used. But this was a case of slaves themselves making the initiative while an indifferent English (and French) population took no action.

The abolitionist movement was still largely confined to England itself, where the political figures Simcoe admired, like Sharp and William Wilberforce, kept lobbying for change. It would take until 1807 for Britain to ban the slave trade and longer than that to free slaves altogether.

Still, Simcoe's legislation was a first for the whole British Empire—an Englishman helping to create Canada for the better, even if it was a mitigated victory.

His legacy, of course, is larger than his role in the anti-slavery movement in Canada. He's personally responsible for choosing the centre of the universe...

Sorry, I mean Toronto.

Simcoe arrived in Upper Canada as its first lieutenant-governor, determined to remake it in Britain's image. He made for a remarkable politician out in the wilderness, enjoying a meal of raccoon when he was required to eat it, his family and his children's nannies temporarily billeted in makeshift tents on the Niagara River while he decided a new capital was needed. Each night, he sang "God Save the King" before he got into bed. He decided this new capital should overlook Lake Ontario and should include streets named after his friends. Yonge, Dundas....

THE RIPPLES THAT STILL FLOW

In Simcoe's Upper Canada, British customs and principles were to be the norm, and he was convinced that disillusioned Americans (closet Anglophiles all, he was sure) would make the trip to the new province if they could get cheap land. Simcoe was sincere, but he sure didn't understand economics. He inadvertently sparked a wave of land speculation and corrupt deals involving property owners who were already established.

His boss was Guy Carleton, now Lord Dorchester, and there was constant friction between the two, with Simcoe resenting how he had little independence. Worn down by political battles and failing health, he left Ontario in 1796.

There's an ironic epilogue to Simcoe's career that most Canadians don't know. Simcoe was sent afterward to be governor of Saint Domingue—Haiti, as it's known today. Inspired by the French Revolution, slaves there rebelled, and under the leadership of Toussaint L'Ouverture, amazingly took over the colony and expelled the French. Even more incredibly, the French royalist planters went to the British in the colonial West Indies, looking for help. Now the abolitionist Simcoe was put in the uncomfortable position of using arms to put slavery back in place.

He had mild military success and told London he was convinced he could capture the whole colony if he received 6000 more troops—London said no. It's intriguing to wonder what reforms he might have put in place if he *had* won, but the slave revolt was a vicious struggle, and as others have noted, Simcoe's heart likely wasn't in fighting oppressed people who were only seeking to win their freedom.

Once again, his poor health was the formal reason that brought him back to England, but perhaps it says something that he was in the political doghouse for having to quit so early (for a while, his superior considered charging him with desertion). Simcoe quit both his position as governor in Saint Domingue and lieutenant-governor for Upper Canada. Later, he was appointed commander-in-chief in India. One wonders what he might have done in that post, but he died in 1806 before he even got the chance to make the journey.

Only decades after Wolfe's conquest, the English were sending out the ripples that would determine how we relate to the French-speaking population of Québec, aboriginal peoples and black Canadians. The waters are deep and sometimes get choppy, and as a country, we still try to navigate them today.

A hurricane from the south in the 19th century would bring us all together, at least for a short while, to steer under an English sail.

"BURNING DOWN THE HOUSE": THE WAR OF 1812

I f anyone thinks the War of 1812 doesn't matter anymore to Canadians, they should talk to writer and artist Douglas Coupland in Vancouver. Or they can always take a stroll near Toronto's Harbourfront, where Coupland's design for a war monument now stands in front of a condominium at Fleet and Bathurst Street. A golden-coloured, four-metre-high British toy soldier stands over a silver American counterpart. The British one wears the uniform of the 1813 Royal Newfoundland Regiment while at his feet lies a member of the 16th U.S. Infantry.

When the monument was unveiled, Coupland explained that he meant it as an elegant way to remind people just who was the victor. "I grew up thinking the Americans lost the War of 1812, and it turns out there's this creeping revisionism happening. Americans are saying maybe we didn't lose. Maybe we won it."

Coupland's unique War of 1812 monument near Fort York in down-town Toronto.

As it turns out, no, they didn't. I find it especially interesting that a *novelist* initiated this project—not a politician, not an academic. Those of us who work in fiction know that sometimes myth is the best way to tell the truth, and if countries need their myths, we in Canada have been raised with a rather sparse diet. Yet we all seem to have a soft spot for the War of 1812, even if we remember few of the details.

We're told the Battle of Vimy Ridge in the Great War was our coming of age, but Vimy was across the sea; World War II, perhaps the most just war in history, was still a crusade on foreign soil. When we say *we* won in 1812, we don't—actually, we can't—forget our side was interchangeable with the English. But this was a war to protect *our* country. The battle on the Plains of Abraham was a dispute within the family, always divisive in the retelling. In contrast, the War of 1812 speaks to us because we get to be the underdog this time, resisting

American arrogance and the presumption that we're a pushover. Surprise! We're not.

I still recall hearing an acquaintance, watching the film *Independence Day* in the theatre, turn to her date as the evil alien spaceship blasted the White House and whisper with delightful malice, "We did it first!"

The causes of the War of 1812 look complicated at first blush, but if you stick with it, the picture comes into focus. To start with, a lot of the blame goes to Napoleon.

While the British and French were already at war, the little Corsican decided to ramp things up after his navy's defeat at Trafalgar, determined to choke off Britain's commercial trade and its naval fleet by seizing ships and threatening third parties who might let those ships into port. Britain retaliated. America's response against all these blockades and counter-blockades was a kind of "self-embargo" of its own waters, as Thomas Jefferson envisioned it. Instead of blaming both sides, Americans singled out Britain for its "outrages"—forgetting that France was also responsible.

The British didn't help their case any by carrying on a practice as if they *did* rule the waves. The Royal Navy, with the full backing of English law, grabbed merchant seamen and fishermen, forcing them to work on its vessels whenever it needed them. Since most Americans had once been British citizens before the Revolution, and they were quite hard to tell apart from the king's own subjects, the press gangs didn't make a distinction. And the American merchant marine complicated things by taking in British deserters. A confrontation on this issue alone was inevitable.

In 1807, when the British ship *Leopold* tried to collect a handful of certain deserters from the American frigate *Chesapeake*, everything had a surreal veneer of politeness to it for a while, with a Royal Navy officer politely making requests through a primitive brass megaphone as the ships floated beside each other. Then another officer rowed over to deliver a dispatch. When he rowed back, he noticed the Americans getting ready for a fight. The British knew better than to sit around watching the gulls, and from a mere 50 metres away, they let their 24-pound (11-kilogram) guns blast into the hull and the rigging of the *Chesapeake*. Three Americans were killed and several other men wounded, and after all that smoke and bloodshed, the British didn't bother to take *other* men they suspected of being deserters but who weren't on their lists. If the Americans needed an excuse to declare war, the British had given them one.

But war still didn't come. Those in power knew they weren't ready, despite the so-called War Hawks who were eager to pick up their rifles and wheel those cannons out.

Added to the American list of grievances was the charge that the British were stirring the Natives up to attack frontier settlements. Now besides the fact that the Native tribes were perfectly able to think for themselves and didn't need anyone to stir them up, the hypocrisy of the American position is staggering. The truth was that American settlers kept encroaching on the Indian territory of the Ohio River. One historian makes a plausible case that these settlers weren't brave pioneers at all—they were just lousy farmers who didn't understand proper crop rotation and were forced to keep looking for arable land because of their own incompetence!

American officials were happy to write up treaties and get worthless signatures from Natives they were pushing out—even though none were ever signed by chiefs of the people who had a legitimate claim to the land, the Shawnee. Indiana's first governor was William Henry Harrison, an egomaniacal, cynical cretin who got Native chiefs drunk before negotiations with them and later got Indiana's prohibition of slavery repealed. (When Harrison became president, he spoke for close to two hours at his inaugural address and rode a white horse in the cold, rainy weather for his parade—he soon fell ill and died, having spent only 30 days in office).

Harrison's ultimate "get" was the Treaty of Fort Wayne in 1809. With a stroke of a pen, he got chiefs of questionable standing to sign over three million acres of land. One specific Native had had enough. This was Tecumseh, the tall, eloquent Native leader who revived the idea that the tribes should unite to face the increasing threat of white expansion. Harrison was happy to have a military showdown, and while he was at it, he used a little Brit-bashing to provoke his countrymen against his preferred enemy. The British, he claimed, were arming the Natives with rifles and powder at their trading posts in preparation for war.

Actually, the British had cut the powder rations for Natives hunting at the frontier posts by a third. True, there were both English and French Canadians who had joined the Natives in skirmishes, whether because they sympathized or expected war to come eventually with the U.S. But officially, Britain was neutral, though sympathetic to the Natives. It had its hands full with Napoleon in Europe.

In November 1811, as tensions increased between the Natives and the Americans, Harrison sent word he wanted to parley to Tecumseh's brother, who had become known as the Prophet after giving up drink and becoming something of a messianic figure for the tribes. The "parley" was a trick. Harrison was moving toward the Native village base of Prophetstown with a force of about 1000 men, Kentucky volunteers and Indiana militia, to annihilate the Natives.

An American deserter tipped off the Natives, who managed to attack first but couldn't hold their ground. After they abandoned their village, Harrison made sure to destroy everything, including the Shawnee's precious granary. Tecumseh came back in the spring to stand "upon the ashes of my own home."

Meanwhile, residents in Washington, DC, must have been going deaf with the clatter of all the sabre ratting. Statements by Americans in Congress demonstrate the U.S. always had a committed if unofficial agenda, and it didn't need a cause for war, just an excuse. Those who wanted to make war on Britain really had nowhere worthwhile to strike except Canada. Halifax was painted as a continuing threat, a base *up there* where British maritime outrages would continue. And those who wanted to gobble up Canada as the latest territorial prize for new settlers found their reasons in British conduct.

Harrison was chomping at the bit for a chance to invade Canada. Henry Clay, the Republican Speaker of the House and the biggest warmonger for a fight with Britain, claimed the militia from his native Kentucky would be enough to take it over. Thomas Jefferson always envisioned a United States expanding across the whole of the continent. When his protegé, President James Madison, finally declared war in June 1812, Jefferson remarked famously, "The acquisition of Canada this year, as far as the neighbourhood of Québec, will be a mere matter of marching."

Not that Jefferson would know. As writer Gore Vidal has tried to point out to his fellow Americans, the author of the Declaration of Independence was always conveniently unavailable when there was any real fighting to be done. Still, Jefferson should have had guessed it wouldn't be that easy—you'd think he'd remember what happened to Benedict Arnold.

The prospects of Canada holding out against invasion didn't look good from the outset. There were fewer than 6000 regulars available in British North America, with only 1200 of those spread very thin at garrisons in Upper Canada. The governor-in-chief, Sir George Prevost, doubted the bulk of the militia could be trusted. He expected scores of men to promptly go over to the enemy, taking their valuable arms with them.

He had even lower expectations of the Aboriginals, despite his lieutenant-governor in Upper Canada believing the Ottawa, the Mississauga, the Mohawk and, of course, the Shawnee would bring thousands of disaffected warriors into the fight. Prevost wrote to London that "hopes of making an effectual defence" counted on being "powerfully assisted from Home." A polite way of saying hurry up, damn it, and send me more men.

But then Prevost, the son of a Swiss officer fighting for the British, was cautious by nature and never expected the embers of American rhetoric to burn into full-scale conflict. If Canada were to survive at all, it would need men of stronger nerve and bolder imagination.

Lucky for us, we got one in Major General Isaac Brock. From a bookish childhood on Guernsey in Britain's Channel Islands, Brock comes into our story as a fascinating, larger-than-life character. Born in the same year as Napoleon and Wellington, 1769, he reportedly had a gentle character yet was a skilled fencer, boxer and swimmer. He also soaked up all the treatises and books on military strategy and tactics he could get his hands on.

"Nothing should be impossible to a soldier," he insisted. "The word impossible should not be found in a soldier's dictionary." ✓

He followed his own credo. When he was a young officer, the horsemen of his regiment in Barbados doubted anyone could ride up the limestone terraces of Mount Hillaby. Brock took his mount all the way up the 1115-foot summit on the eastern flank.

We know he was clever and smart on his feet by an episode that occurred when he was a young ensign. A regiment bully who was a crack shot challenged Brock to a duel. Brock had grown to well over six feet tall (close to two metres) when the usual height for men in this age was still about five and a half (less than 1.7 metres); he would have made a big target. Brock accepted the challenge—with the caveat that they shoot across the width of a handkerchief. In other word, inches from each other, point-blank! The bully backed down and later quit the regiment in embarrassment.

Brock had seen action in Europe and got to meet Horatio Nelson. Brock had missed death when a musket ball stuck in the silk scarves around his neck. He was the man to watch, an officer advancing rapidly up through the ranks. But Canada was a disappointment, a backwater to him, and he wrote to his family about

Isaac Brock: arguably, the first national war hero for all Canadians

"the uninteresting and insipid life I am doomed to lead in this retirement."

He was wrong. It would get very interesting, sometimes in disturbing shades. He believed in discipline and once chased six deserters in an open boat across Lake Ontario into American territory to get them back. Worse was the case of a planned mutiny in late 1803 at Fort George, foiled by a message to Brock naming the lead conspirators. It soon emerged that his second-in-command, Roger Sheaffe, was unpopular for busting men down in rank over paltry infractions. Brock chastised him for this behaviour and considered Sheaffe to have "little knowledge of mankind."

After the obligatory court martial when Brock
addressed the mutineers, knowing they had to be exe-
cuted, his voice broke with feeling. One of them was
moved to say, "Had you commanded us, Sir, this never
would have occurred." The subsequent execution, held
in Montréal, was a botched affair in which some soldiers
fired early while others fired too late and too far away.
The condemned men—wounded and in agony lashed
against poles—all needed a hasty coup de grace. It was an
ugly business that disgusted Brock. He was a soldier, but
one who clearly didn't believe in needless loss of life.

The mutineer's comment is also telling. Brock must
have had a particular charisma, because a lieutenant
remembers he "had a peculiar habit of attaching all parties
and people to his person; in short, he infused the most
unbounded confidence in all ranks and descriptions of
men under his command." For a war hero who's remembered for his charm at parties and with women, no biographer has persuasively pinned him down as having
a specific lover or fiancée. What has come down to us is
what seemed to be a genuine, if brief, friendship and col-
laboration with Tecumseh. "A more sagacious or a more
gallant warrior does not, I believe, exist," Brock wrote of
the Shawnee chief. When Tecumseh met Brock, he looked
to his followers and declared, "This is a man!"

A man like this would find defeatism incredibly
frustrating, and Brock did. Before war was declared,
he urged Prevost to let him conduct a few pre-emptive
strikes, but his boss countered with some justification
that this was the kind of incident the War Hawks would
jump on. Prevost liked Brock but considered him reckless.
When war at last came, he expected the main fight to be
in Québec and so only boosted Brock's forces in Upper
Canada by 500 men.

To add to Brock's headaches was the infuriating attitude of the legislative assembly in York. Here were the
Americans marching on their way, and legislators
decided their main priority was...a school bill. "A full
belief possesses them all that this province must inevitably
succumb," wrote Brock. He had the chamber dismissed
and promptly got on with the work of preparing for
uninvited guests.

The man the Americans pinned their hopes of conquest
on was Brigadier General William Hull, once a hero of the
Revolution and now closing in on 60. You have to seri-
ously wonder at Hull's intelligence. Though Madison
instructed him to send his army across the Detroit River
as soon as possible for the war's outbreak, it took him
weeks to mobilize his force 300 kilometres south of Fort
Detroit. When Jefferson made his quip about marching,
he probably didn't imagine a miserable rain-soaked
parade of men plodding through thick mud across an
area called Black Swamp.

What Hull did next was truly idiotic. Some accounts
point out that the messages informing him the war had
been formally declared arrived late. It hardly mattered.
Here was a general who already knew his country *would*
declare war and who had been sent with the specific
purpose to get into position to take full advantage of
this imminent fact. So what did he do?

On July 1, he chartered the American schooner *Cuyahoga*
to carry his men (sick from the arduous march), his officers' baggage, his musicians and his own personal papers
up Lake Erie to Fort Detroit. When he learned the war
was on, Hull panicked and rushed men off to overtake
the *Cuyahoga*. Too late. Brock had sent a warning letter
to the British as early as June 25, and redcoat soldiers in
a longboat, armed with sabres and pickaxes, captured the

schooner. Thanks to Hull's own stupidity, the British now knew exactly how many men were coming and his exact invasion plan. The Provincial Marine lieutenant in charge of the operation even made the American band play "God Save the King."

Hull crossed the Detroit River anyway, invading Canada at Windsor (the British called it Sandwich at the time) with a force mostly comprised of militiamen. Many stayed behind, acting on their constitutional right not to serve on foreign soil. After occupying the town and meeting no trouble, Hull arranged for a proclamation to be issued, one that announced, "Inhabitants of Canada! After thirty years of peace and prosperity, the United States have been driven to arms." After promising to protect the rights and property of Canadians who had felt Britain's "tyranny" and seen her "injustice," Hull made his own position crystal clear, "If, contrary to your own interests and the just expectation of my country, you should take part in the approaching contest, you will be considered and treated as enemies, and the horrors and calamities of war will stalk before you." Those who fought with Natives were promised "instant destruction."

Nothing like a threat of extermination to confirm that you were being rescued.

From Fort George, Brock issued his own coolly worded proclamation in response, one that reads today more like a newspaper editorial than a rallying cry, but nevertheless must have spoken to the mood of the settlers. Early on, Brock's needle of logic stabs Hull's pompous balloon: "The officer commanding that detachment has thought proper to invite His Majesty's subjects, not merely to a quiet and unresisting submission, but insults them with a cell to seek voluntarily the protection of his government." Brock must have understood that those who stayed in Canada wanted an alternative to the States; they weren't yearning to be acquired. "Where is the Canadian subject who can truly affirm to himself that he has been injured by the government, in his person, his property, or his liberty? Where is to be found, in any part of the world, a growth so rapid in prosperity and wealth, as this colony exhibits?"

Thanks to captured dispatches and correspondence, Brock had insight into his opponent's character, and he realized he was dealing with a man weak in resolve, fearful of Native "savages." (Hull had written to the Secretary of War about his concern over being surrounded by "Indians.") Brock would have made an excellent poker player. Demanding Hull's surrender in a note, he let his enemy know that "you must be aware, that the numerous body of Indians who have attached themselves to my troops will be beyond all control the moment the contest commences." Hull was concerned enough to deploy the rest of his militia around the town in case of a night attack. Brock then decided to up the bluff.

His aide, Major Thomas Evans, had the idea to dress the militia in old redcoat uniforms, making it appear that Brock had a larger force of regulars. Meanwhile, Tecumseh had his warriors go around in a circle three times past the fort. Just as the battle was about to get underway, a flag of surrender was offered. Hull asked for a three-day respite from the hostilities. Brock answered that if the Americans didn't hand over the fort in three hours, he "would blow up every one of them." By ten in the morning, the Union Jack was flying over Fort Detroit.

The Americans were so shocked by the surrender that they court-martialled Hull for cowardice and ordered his execution. He was convinced to the end he had saved

Detroit from a Native massacre. Madison gave Hull a pardon, but his career was in tatters. As for Canada, Brock's victory was an inspiration. "The disaffected are silenced," Brock wrote his brothers back home, and now the militia actually believed they had a chance.

If Brock had got his way, he would have chased Americans deep into Michigan, but once again Prevost was the voice of caution, trying to negotiate an armistice. The hero who captured Detroit was shaking his head in frustration, knowing the Americans weren't going to be reasonable "without the aid of a sword" and that if only he were given the signal, he could capture more territory. "I firmly believe that I could at this moment sweep everything before me from Fort Niagara to Buffalo."

Prevost was in his way, as he would be in the way of others in the future. Instead, the sleepy, battered tortoise of the American army had all of September to get into position for revenge.

One rainy night in mid-October, sentries on Queenston Heights heard a terrible racket coming from across the Niagara River at Lewiston. The Americans were supposed to be boarding boats to row across to the Canadian side. What happened that evening was Monty Python slapstick. Some fool had placed all the oars into one longboat—which happened to be the one getting swept downstream by the current! When the wayward boat finally ran aground, the single officer on it blundered into the woods. The assault was delayed a couple of days.

On October 13, the Americans tried again but still hadn't learned their lesson, or rather the right one. This time they had oars, but overloaded their boats, and they didn't have boats large enough to carry their heavy guns. Almost half of them sank or were carried away by the current, and as if that weren't bad enough, many militia-men, especially New Yorkers, refused again to cross onto foreign soil.

Across the river, British soldiers—who learned drill, drill and more drill—were mowing down the Americans with musket fire before many could get their feet on dry land. The British soldier was expected to fire off at least two musket rounds a minute. Now consider what goes into loading and firing a musket, and you realize how amazing that is.

The cannons were Brock's wake-up call at Fort George, and by the time he and his aide, Lieutenant Colonel John Macdonnell, reached Queenston on horseback it was dawn. The Americans pinned below the Heights managed to find a winding fisherman's path farther along that led up the cliff. If this sounds familiar, it should. Brock—who had been stationed in Montréal, who had been reared on Wolfe's legend as a boy and who studied tactics—was getting tricked the same way Montcalm had been at the Plains of Abraham. And he was about to make Montcalm's same mistake.

Macdonnell launched an attack against the Americans with two companies of militia and drove them back, but then he was fatally wounded and the Americans managed to get reinforcements from below. Had he been smart, Brock would have retreated at this point to wait for his own reinforcements from Fort George. As Montcalm had done before him, he decided not to wait. He gathered his men, and dressed in his bright red uniform and wearing a garish scarf that was a gift from Tecumseh, he held his sword in the air and launched an attack up the hill.

When he saw a few men turning tail, he barked in disgust, "This is the first time I have ever seen the 49th turn their backs!" This shamed the ranks into closing up and carrying on. Up the slick grass they went, running, panting, sometimes stumbling, but gaining ground and hearing their commander give the order to fix bayonets and charge.

Then there was the crack of a musket, and Brock dropped, hit by an American hiding in the bushes. A teen-age Canadian militia soldier rushed up to his fallen commander and asked, "Are you much hurt, Sir?" Brock couldn't answer. He was dead.

It was the Natives and, oddly enough, the detested Major General Roger Sheaffe who saved the day for the Canadian side. About 300 Native warriors kept the Americans busy on the west, which allowed Sheaffe to take his time and patiently outflank his enemy. When Sheaffe's regulars charged, many of the Americans threw themselves off the cliffs, fearing torture and scalping by the Natives.

Brock's body lay in state for three days, and then he was given a joint funeral with Macdonnell that one observer considered "the grandest and most solemn" ever seen in Upper Canada. When British cannon fired their 21-gun salute, the American guns across the river at Fort Niagara and Lewiston fired in a respectful matching tribute to the enemy general.

We've spent time on Isaac Brock because he is *the* Canadian icon of the war. His victory at Detroit prompted a 180-degree turn in Canadian attitudes. He blew away a fog of defeatism that blocked clear thinking. Who knows what he might have accomplished had he lived? Today, it's often pointed out that he, perhaps, never really trusted Canadians, certainly not those in the militia, and his preference was for the glory of a European posting. On these grounds, some argue, he doesn't qualify as a Canadian hero.

This is the annoying kind of reductive, self-effacing logic this country too often brings to its champions (another inherited English trait—building 'em up to tear 'em down). In his sympathy for the rights of the Natives, Brock is reminiscent of one of Canada's later figures, Major James Walsh of the Mounties who befriended Sitting Bull. In his pragmatism and compassion to avoid needless loss of life, he's right up there with Great War-general Arthur Currie.

Now go back and read the lines Brock wrote in response to Hull. They bear repeating: "*Where is to be found, in any part of the world, a growth so rapid in prosperity and wealth, as this colony exhibits?*" Brock was a military man. He could have made a different kind of propaganda appeal to maintain discipline and keep order, one that instilled fear or made threats. But no, he made his case on the colony's merits and his own sincere admiration for Natives such as Tecumseh fighting for their home. It would be inaccurate to think he ever identified himself with these settlers or thought in terms of our national identity. Yes, he was an Englishman. But by choice of conscience and his own sense of duty, he fought for Canada and so deserves to be considered a legitimate *Canadian* hero.

Besides the burning of the White House, Canadians also vaguely remember that the Americans came up to burn York. I've heard many people mix up the two events, as if York came *after* Washington as an American reprisal—it didn't. And as it happened, the burning of York didn't turn out exactly as the Americans planned or hoped. One of the strangest aspects of the capture was that the British helped. That's right, the British even helped burn the provincial capital.

The Royal Navy had concentrated on holding the seas, which left the Americans gradually getting the upper hand in the Great Lakes. One of the ironies of the war was that for all the much-vaunted English sea power, the Americans did fairly well on the lakes while often having less success on land.

The U.S. Secretary of War John Armstrong wanted to go after Kingston and York and wreck their shipping and shipbuilding works. His logic was that this would ensure control of Lake Ontario and the Niagara Peninsula and would give the Americans their first step to taking over Upper Canada.

In charge of the land forces was Major General Henry Dearborn, yet another revolutionary veteran past his prime and unhealthily obese. During the attack on York, a couple of soldiers had to wheel him around in a cart because no one could find a horse and carriage. He also seemed to suffer from "Hull's disease." Dearborn was *sure* that Prevost had close to 7000 men poised to attack the American-held Sackets Harbor in a couple of days or so, and he timidly recommended that the assault target York instead of Kingston. Like Hull for Detroit, Dearborn dithered, wasting March and April to gather his men at Sackets Harbor.

Dearborn also was similarly victimized by bad weather. Ships that were tossed about on rough seas finally dumped the poor seasick Americans—their general included—at their landing point early one morning like so many half-drowned rats. Dearborn handed command over to the younger and sturdier 34-year-old brigadier general, Zebulon Pike. Up on the Scarborough Bluffs, British sentries had spotted the American ships approach the day before, but Roger Sheaffe didn't seize the opportunity to organize his few men properly for a counter-assault. After three hours the British pulled back, and then a gunner accidentally dropped his match on a wooden chest full of gun magazines. Men were blown to bits, with one of the pitiful wounded even brought to the surgeon in a wheelbarrow.

Sheaffe decided to retreat and take his men to Kingston. On leaving, he had one of the ships being built, *Sir Isaac Brock*, set afire; he could have let it fall into American hands since the construction work was apparently incompetent. He also ordered the large powder magazine to be blown up, denying the Americans this prize as well. It did more than that. Soldiers in the Royal Newfoundland Regiment turned to see "an immense cloud," the blast killing 40 Americans and wounding 200 others. One of the dead was Pike, his head smashed in by falling debris as he was interrogating a prisoner. Surgeons "waded in blood, cutting off arms, legs, and trepanning heads."

There's a silly legend that Grenadier Pond in Toronto's High Park is named after retreating soldiers who drowned as they ran across the pond and fell through the ice. This is nonsense. The assault on York happened toward the end of April, and anyone familiar with a Toronto spring knows there would have been no ice. (The name of the pond actually comes from later in the century when soldiers used to fish there.)

However the British retreated, they had cost the Americans much, and it's been pointed out that Sheaffe could have taken advantage of the magazine explosion to regroup and counter-attack. He didn't, and he'd have to explain himself later to Prevost. On the American side, with Pike's death imminent, Dearborn reassumed command, but the horror of the explosion had provoked his soldiers, and military discipline soon broke down.

The Americans burned Government House and the military barracks and destroyed the government printing press. Under the capitulation agreement, private property was supposed to be respected, but the U.S. soldiers went on a rampage, looting homes and bullying civilians. Britons who were let out of jail and certain lowlifes joined in. So the pillaging can't be completely blamed on the Americans.

The defeat of York was a punishing blow to morale. Its capture and burning, however, never left a lasting psychological impact on Canadians, not in the same way our reprisal was a blow to Americans. Washington was, after all, their national capital. York's development wasn't nearly on the same scale—it boasted a population of less than 1000 citizens. And let's face it, if you took a poll today, you'd probably find folks in Edmonton and Regina ready to volunteer to burn down Toronto.

Where the war *really* had a lasting, constructive impact on the urban landscape wasn't in Upper Canada at all, but in Halifax. British sea power, combined with the natural defences of the city's harbour, limited the risks while allowing Halifax to reap all the dividends from privateers preying on American vessels—and from the navy bringing in goods and captured ships. Nothing helps local capitalism so much as when you're spending somebody else's capital.

When the war was over, there were legitimate concerns the city would shrink back to its dull trough, one that seemed to be a part of a boom-and-bust cycle tied to conflicts like the revolution or the Seven Years' War. The British launched a costly public works program to try to keep that from happening.

But in 1813, war was to Halifax what oil would be later for Calgary. This is how one city editor put it: "Happy state of Nova Scotia! Amongst all this tumult we have lived in peace and security; invaded only by a numerous host of doubloons and dollars."

One of the prizes towed in was the *Chesapeake*, and the story of its capture made perfect grist for Patrick O'Brian's book, *The Fortune of War*, one of his Aubrey–Maturin series of Royal Navy novels (cracking good fiction—more historical accuracy, less waving around of cutlasses than you get in the movies). The capture of this prize happened at the best time possible. The Royal Navy was suffering severe embarrassment because its blockade failed to prevent a couple of American ships from slipping through. Worse, the Brits hadn't performed very well so far, if you can believe it, in naval battles against American vessels. They badly needed a "win." And they got one with British Captain Philip Broke of the *Shannon,* whose ship wasn't nearly as big as the *Chesapeake*. He was about to prove that size doesn't matter—at least not when you're hauling around cannons on the Atlantic.

Broke had been training his gun crew for weeks—and with live ammunition. He also paid for gun sights and other aiming devices out of his own pocket. The good captain of the *Shannon* was definitely a belt *and* suspenders fellow, and he was bound and determined to be ready for an engagement. As Broke's ship sat outside Boston harbour, he sent a polite message to his opposite number, Captain James Lawrence of the *Chesapeake,* to "try the fortunes of our respective flags." This is as nasty as trash talk got between gentleman officers of the 19th century. No one talked about your mama, it was: Would you be good enough, dear fellow, to sail out so I can blast you to smithereens? If you please.

Broke didn't need to bother. As it happened, even before his message arrived, the *Chesapeake* was heading toward him. This showed more confidence than Lawrence actually had. He had doubts about his inexperienced crew, and just before he went up on deck, he wrote a quick note in his cabin to a friend, asking him to take care of his family.

The two ships moved around each other for position, and by late afternoon they both opened fire. Broke's relentless crew training paid off, and his first blast was devastating. Each ship had 38 guns, and after blasting holes in each other, they collided, with the *Shannon*'s after-port getting snagged by the *Chesapeake*'s anchor. But that put the American ship's decks squarely in front of the British guns. After another crippling blast, British sailors jumped onto the American decks with their blades out and muskets firing. Lawrence was wounded twice—once by a sniper's shot to his leg and then he took another hit in the chest. As he saw the British pouring onto the *Chesapeake*, he stood up as best he could and shouted, "Don't give up the ship! Don't give up the ship!"

That sounds all very noble and heroic, and the Americans lauded him as a hero, but in fact, his crew *did* give up the ship—despite his express orders for them to fight to the end. Easy for him to say—he lay dying in his cabin. The ranking American officer on deck told his men to lay down their arms after 15 minutes of vicious hand-to-hand combat.

Broke suffered a severe cutlass wound to his head but would live, achieving fame as a hero second only to Horatio Nelson. There were cheers in Halifax as the *Chesapeake* was towed into its harbour, and you can still see artifacts from the ship in the city's Maritime Museum of the Atlantic.

Despite such a heady victory, there were equally humiliating failures. In the autumn of 1813, when the Americans fought the army of General Henry Proctor for control of Lake Erie, Tecumseh was disgusted by the British commander choosing to retreat. So, for that matter, were the British soldiers, who didn't think Proctor was very good at his job. They were owed plenty of back pay and were running out of ammunition and food. Tecumseh threw Proctor's words back in his face with some justification. "You always told us that you would never draw your foot off British ground." He compared Proctor's withdrawal to "a fat animal that carries its tail upon its back; but when affrighted it drops it between its legs and runs off."

When Proctor finally had to stand and fight near Chatham, the British lines broke, and his men ran into the woods. It was Tecumseh who held fast, yelling for his Native warriors to keep on firing. One has to wonder if he didn't think of Brock at some point in his last moments, feeling betrayed by what he considered Proctor's cowardice and knowing it could have gone so differently with another man to lead these whites. He died in battle, along with his dream of a Native confederacy united against American expansionism.

The war had devolved into a stalemate. The Americans were shocked when they failed to take Montréal, getting beaten back by French Canadians at the Battle of Chateauguay, and by late 1813, they were wondering how to get out of this whole mess they started. The war would give birth to the image of Uncle Sam and "the rockets' red glare" in a shrill national anthem annoyingly sung before every concert and football game, but at the time, it was a highly unpopular conflict in the United States. As it continued into 1814, the U.S. Congress only agreed to authorize $25 million for the war effort. The American negotiators knew they were in trouble. By now Napoleon had been dumped on Elba, and the British forces were free to come over to North America to settle the score.

Albert Gallatin, who as the U.S. Secretary of the Treasury had made a case for war, sailed to Europe as one of the leaders of the delegation to broker a peace. He got a jolt to his complacency while staying in London, discovering that far from worn down by the years of war, "the English people eagerly wish that their pride may be fully gratified by what they call the 'punishment of America.'"

But the English weren't taking the Americans to the woodshed—they were only meeting them in Ghent, Holland. And though they knew they were in a strong position, when the two sides sat down together in August, it looked like the British were prepared to be reasonable. They didn't want to talk about impressment—the Royal Navy practice of press gangs and of searching ships for deserters, the very thing that touched off the conflict—but they knew the Americans would, so they were willing to listen. They considered a certain land issue far more important. Britain's Foreign Secretary, Viscount Castlereagh, gave his firm backing to the protection "which the Indians, as allies, are entitled to claim at our hands."

This good intention, of course, only went so far and had the predictable paternalism. There were, after all, no Natives sitting at the table in Ghent negotiating for their stakes in the game (there were no French or English Canadians either). British protection of the Natives wasn't completely altruistic; there was a potential tactical benefit of a buffer zone between the United States and Canada. But Castlereagh was sincere, at least for a while, in suggesting both Britain and America place their relationships "with each other, as well as with several Indian nations, upon a footing of less jealousy and irritation."

The chief American negotiator was John Quincy Adams. Intense and deeply neurotic, a bookish, brilliant lawyer and patriot, Adams was many things, but he was not the gentle genius played by Anthony Hopkins in *Amistad*. He flew into a lather over a dispute about where in Ghent the negotiations would be held. As the talks moved into September, Adams crafted disingenuous arguments to avoid the notion that the Natives get their own country—these hunter-gatherers roamed where they will and never settled. To give them a country was pointless. The United States, on the other hand, had to expand as its numbers increased.

Britain's negotiator, Henry Goulburn, knew where this logic was going and asked how Britain could guarantee Canada's security. "A liberal and amicable course of policy toward America," Adams shot back. The code wasn't difficult for Goulburn to crack. If you're not around, we will take what we want if it's not freely given.

Goulburn was an evangelical Christian and Anglophile with complete faith in the Empire's civilizing mission, and even he balked at this unapologetic air of sweeping entitlement. His personal opinion of Adams was that he was a bully. Throughout much of the negotiations, the British accused the United States of always having the secret goal of annexing Canada. The Americans blustered denials, claiming it was one thing for their congressmen or senators to express ambitions of conquest, but no formal intent ever existed on government documents.

You couldn't blame the British for spotting a credibility gap when Henry Clay, the man who was picked as Speaker of the House on his very first day in the chamber and one of the loudest voices for taking over Canada, was sitting right there in Ghent as a member of the American delegation.

John Quincy Adams, of course, was later one of the architects of the Monroe Doctrine, which presumed the entire American continent was within its sphere of influence and Europe should keep its hands off.

While Adams was in Ghent insisting the United States have breathing room, he didn't know that his fellow Americans across the Atlantic were panting for breath, running for their lives in Washington. It was payback time for the burning of York.

Twenty warships of the Royal Navy prowled Chesapeake Bay for days, terrifying Americans over just where the British would land. The Secretary of War, John Armstrong, had considered Baltimore far more strategically important and had done little to fortify the national capital. Despite this, when the British finally attacked Washington, their 4000 troops faced 7000 Americans. But the good news was that only a quarter of those were regulars, and the strongest resistance ended up coming from 400 sailors under Commodore Joshua Barney. They had brought up guns stripped from their vessels.

It was a sweltering 40° C, and President James Madison and his Cabinet were on horseback, all soaked in sweat.

Generals squabbled over who had the authority to organize defensive positions. The British soon put an end to that racket. They used rockets, each of which carried an impressive 32-pound (14.5 kilograms) explosive and made a hell of a lot of noise, but didn't do much damage. In terms of spreading panic, however, they did a great job. Within half an hour of the first blast, the American militiamen were sprinting from the field, leaving Commodore Barney's sailors to hold the line.

"Never did men with arms in their hands make better use of their legs," quipped one British officer.

The fleeing president got back to the White House by half-past four and discovered his dinner meal cooling on a table and his wife gone. Dolly Madison had left in a wagon packed with velvet curtains, silverware, boxes of papers and books and a portrait of George Washington cut out of its frame. President Madison got on a horse and rode with a small party for the government's fallback position in Virginia, glimpsing the capital on fire as he took the road of retreat.

Canadians like to think that the reason it's called the White House is because we burned it, and the legend goes that a coat of white paint was hurriedly applied later to the charred mansion. It's an amusing thought, but it just ain't so. The term "White House" was apparently in use before the war, and the presidential mansion was always white. What the British *did* do was help themselves to the presidential Madeira, swipe some shirts to exchange for their sweaty ones and help themselves to a few keepsakes before they set fire to the curtains and furniture and gutted the structure.

Unlike the rampage and looting in York, there was an odd English restraint to the burning of Washington.

The British were quite specific in their targets for arson, choosing only government buildings—the Capitol, the Treasury, the War Office and, of course, the White House. In fact, at around midnight on the evening right after the battle, a couple of women pleaded with Rear Admiral George Cockburn not to set alight the offices of the government paper, *The National Intelligencer*—they were afraid their building would catch fire as well. Cockburn chivalrously complied, having men burn the newspaper's contents, instead, in a bonfire on the street. When another group of women came by, Cockburn and his men chatted up the ladies and served them refreshments.

If Canadians take a mischievous pleasure in the burning of the White House, they should enjoy even more the idea that the U.S. president and the army officers ran for their lives, and our side drank their liquor and had a chance to get lucky with their receptive women.

Despite the flames that impressed Madison riding to Virginia, few private structures were put to the torch or even vandalized. Instead, the British went about disposing of tonnes of military hardware. When they quit the capital and sailed out from Benedict, Maryland, they took away 200 guns, 500 barrels of powder and thousands of musket cartridges. Worse, they had dealt the Americans a psychological blow, and recalling how their enemy ran off the field, dubbed the battle "The Bladensburg Races."

You would think the news about Washington would be devastating to the inflexible American negotiators, and for a short time the Brits pressed the advantage to try to make some breakthroughs over the Native question. But the truth was that the British were losing interest in North America. Things had not been going so well with Russia after the fall of Napoleon, France was restless, and those in London were far away from knowing what was actually happening in Halifax and York. The situation still seemed to be a stalemate. After the Washington victory came a British defeat at Plattsburgh—the timid Prevost had been directly in charge.

The British softened their stance over the Natives. Then they tried to get the Duke of Wellington to go over and fix things. Wellington replied that, sure, he'd go if he was ordered...not that he'd probably be able to do much good. The key, he shrewdly pointed out, was to take the Great Lakes. "Till that superiority is acquired, it is impossible...to keep the enemy out of the whole frontier, much less to make any conquest from the enemy." Get a good peace deal, advised Wellington. "You can get no territory: indeed, the state of your military operations, however creditable, does not entitle you to demand any."

The British kept on pushing the matter of the Lakes. The Americans never budged. It's hard not to believe that had the war gone on with a talented commander like Wellington in charge (rather than the incompetent Prevost), the political landscape of North America might look different today. By October 1814, the U.S. government was close to bankrupt and its navy couldn't pay its sailors. Madison couldn't get war loans to finance increases in the militia.

In Ghent, the American negotiators had been cooped up together for months and were gnawing on each other's delicate nerves. Relations were almost as tense when the Americans tried to socialize with the Brits. The Americans considered the British boring; the British found the Americans vulgar, with lousy table manners.

A lack of English will, however, sealed Canada's fate more than anything else. Both sides were weary, and the dejected Americans dropped the issue of impressment altogether. With the negotiations now crawling into December, the British wanted to get back to matters of Europe. At first, they suggested both sides hang onto what each had gained in the conflict. In the end, the solution was to turn back the clock to how things stood in 1811, but that gave the Americans more territory and didn't solve the security question of the Great Lakes.

By 1818, a new treaty cut a line across the 49th Parallel to decide the border between the U.S. and Canada. Oregon took a little longer to sort out, but the start of our national boundaries really starts with the War of 1812. It also marks an incredible betrayal by the British of the Natives' sovereignty. They all but abandoned the Native peoples to their fate. During the negotiations, Britain's Henry Goulburn complained to John Quincy Adams about how American expansionism was pushing Natives from their lands into British provinces. They wound up encroaching on the territory of Natives already occupying the land. Adams cavalierly dismissed this, replying he had "never heard of any complaint of this kind before."

So there were to be no checks on America taking the West from the Natives; no Native buffer state to give Canada relief either. With the English refusal to stand up for the Natives in Ghent, Canada eventually chose a different path to stop American encroachment. It decided on its own expansion west and a disastrous slow-death policy of assimilation for the Natives.

When the treaty was first announced, both the American and British negotiators were heavily critized on their home fronts. Americans complained they didn't get much out of the treaty. The British were sore they didn't punish the Americans as expected. Canadians also felt they had been let down and were stuck with a bad agreement. Opinions gradually changed. It took weeks for the news of the treaty to spread, and in the meantime, the Americans managed to win the Battle of New Orleans. This quickly got turned into the "battle that won the war" when it did nothing of the kind—it just kept the British out of Louisiana. Across the Atlantic, the British wiped their foreheads with relief that Wellington had been kept in Europe after Napoleon escaped from Elba.

In Canada, a myth took form that the British didn't save the province at all; it was a plucky home-grown militia that fought the good fight. It wasn't true, but it made folks feel better.

Which just leaves the question: who won? Canadian historian Bruce Hutchison summed it up in a neat line by writing, "The United States had lost a war and won a conference." The more glib Will Ferguson echoes this view that the Americans won, pulling out the old saw that war is a political tool. But he somewhat misses the point. Both politically and militarily, the Americans didn't reach their goal of taking us over.

Sorry, Americans, we won the war. That's not just because a Canadian is saying it. Donald R. Hickey, who was a professor of Military History at the U.S. Army Command and General Staff College, as well as a visiting professor at the U.S. Naval War College, also says it. He calls Canada the big winner "because it resisted the American embrace, retained its British connection, and thus laid the foundation for its future independence and nationhood."

That wraps it up nicely, but the War of 1812 had a far more profound impact than that. What was our foundation? Just what were we becoming? In his masterful study, *For Honour's Sake*, Mark Zuehlke points out that the motley collection of French Canadians, British settlers, Loyalist exiles and American immigrants all found common ground. "If they were not yet Canadian, they were not American. Had they desired to be so, the war provided ample opportunity to align themselves with the invading forces.... Instead, a majority had supported the British resistance to American invasion."

So yes, we weren't fully formed, but in the first test of survival the tiny communities and infant institutions of the two Canadas and of the flourishing Maritimes managed to hold their own. There were great gains in the war, and had the English at home not been continually distracted by affairs in continental Europe, they might have conducted stronger negotiations to hang onto those gains or chosen to teach the Americans a serious lesson about predatory expansionism. Emphasis on *might*. Of course, we'll never know. And for every timid Prevost, we did have better men like Brock.

Yes, we're back to that dubious *we* again, for the paradox of Englishness in Canadian culture truly starts here. When we say "we" won the War of 1812, it sounds a little bit odd, and even if you flew out of Gatwick or Heathrow yesterday, your connection to those who won is rather distant—if you're British, you'd have to do your homework before you found an ancestor who was here. If you count yourself among the Canadian "we," well, who you are today is at best a descendant of the winners, and you're something else entirely.

It's a paradox. An Italian who takes pride in Giovanni Caboto still feels Italian at the end of the day: food, language, music…. But an English Canadian doesn't quite have that same link with culture unless it's nourished through family ties. Instead, our heritage has found expression through nationalism.

Ironically, as our Englishness diluted, the English victories of 1812 became more of a shared accomplishment for all Canadians.

WITHIN
THE BOSOM OF
A SINGLE STATE

On May 18, 1838, the coronation was held for another German, this time 19-year-old Queen Victoria of the House of Saxe-Coburg and Gotha. She became the first royal resident at Buckingham Palace. On the throne for 63 years, her name would become synonymous with an age. But in the first 10 years of her reign, government ministers such as Robert Peel, who wanted to defy her, and Lord Palmerston, who chose to outright ignore her, drove her to distraction.

If Britain's Victoria found Parliament frustrating, across the Atlantic her subjects found it downright maddening. It was a bizarre turnabout: the constitutional monarch had limited power, yet her appointed governors in the Canadas ruled like kings, making crucial decisions for the English elite while the elected assemblies were almost reduced to pointless talking shops. When Canadians found the situation intolerable,

Viceroys!

they started twin rebellions. Both were doomed to be put down.

On the exact same day the crown was placed on Victoria's head, her governor general across the sea, an Englishman named John George Lambton, allowed 150 Patriotes of the Lower Canada Rebellion out of prison, giving them amnesty as he tried to tease out the puzzle of colonial grievances. Lambton didn't stay in Canada very long, and yet his impact was considerable, his opinions still controversial. It's because of him that two Canadas became one.

What happened to all that proto-nationalistic spirit from the War of 1812 and in the 1780s? Québec politician Joseph Papineau had run military dispatches for Guy Carleton during the American Revolution. French Canadians had fought valiantly during the Battle of Châteauguay in the War of 1812. But only a little more than two decades later, journalists were sending editorial broadsides against the provincial assembly, and Papineau's son, Louis-Joseph, was preaching republicanism and suggesting Lower Canada would be better off if it split away and joined the United States.

The truth is that the concessions in the age of James Murray and Guy Carleton that were intended to placate the Québecois—and more importantly, keep them in check—had become an entrenched system of corruption that was literally retarding the progress of a people. Roads and schools didn't get built. Why spend the money there? Land tenancy was exorbitant and downright medieval. The French stayed in their areas, and the wealthier English lived in their own enclaves. The Roman

Catholic Church tightened its grip on the province's education system. Now this is important, because by perpetuating all this, the English would suffer an extraordinary whirlwind in the late 20th century.

An observation on Lower Canada from Alexis de Tocqueville, that 19th-century French historian and chronicler of *Democracy in America*, rings disturbingly familiar: "Although French is the most commonly spoken language, most newspapers, notices and even the commercial signs of French merchants are in English."

The chickens would eventually come home to roost.

In the 1830s, residents in Lower Canada knew change would only come if their provincial assembly had teeth. Life was very different in York, now renamed Toronto, which had come a long way from Simcoe's wilderness to boast gas lamps and paved sidewalks. But the complaint was the same. A Scottish publisher who always enjoyed a good political or legal fight, William Lyon Mackenzie, complained, "One great excellence of the English constitution consists in the limits it imposes on the will of a king, by requiring responsible men to give effect to it." But in Upper Canada, Mackenzie saw the lieutenant-governor and the British Parliament leaving "the representative branch of the legislature powerless and dependent."

These are just a couple of lines from a thick book of protest Mackenzie sent to London. Joseph Papineau in Lower Canada was more concise, whittling down his grievances for the British government to Ninety-Two Resolutions. It hardly mattered—London chose to ignore both documents. It had seen this kind of thing before with 13 irascible American colonies. If it expected the grumbling to fade away, it was dead wrong, because by late 1837, rebels were drilling outside Toronto.

In Montréal, Papineau's Patriotes were even more militant and threatened militia officers who didn't want to join their cause.

The Lower Canada Rebellion can never be painted as a purely French versus British affair. One of its main architects was an English doctor and a distant relative of Horatio Nelson. Like many a convert, Wolfred Nelson started by fanatically despising what he later embraced: Catholics and French Canadians. He wound up marrying one and raising their children in her faith. Perhaps it was his service in the militia in 1813 that changed his attitudes; he was the only English officer in an all-French battalion, getting a chance to see Québecois fight to keep Lower Canada British.

More than two decades later, he listened to the firebrand Papineau whip up a crowd for support, not far from where he had served in the Richelieu Valley. Nelson got his own chance to address the Patriotes and told them, "I say that the time has come to melt down our dishes and tin spoons to make bullets."

In mid-November 1837, the Patriotes were ready to declare the independence of Lower Canada as arrest warrants went out for Papineau and Nelson. Anticipating that the rebels might start something, British troops were sent to St. Denis, where Nelson was holed up in a village house behind a stone wall. He had been tipped off about the attack and was quite ready to engage his enemy, telling his men, "A bit of courage, and victory will be ours."

This could have been wishful thinking. After all, he faced a veteran commander of the Napoleonic Wars, a Colonel Charles Gore, who led seasoned British troops while Nelson had a ragtag crew of Québecois farmers and tradesmen. The French were good snipers, but what really forced the British to retreat was the weather and plain old fatigue. They had marched through freezing rain and mud during the night and were exhausted. After six hours of fighting, Gore ordered them to retreat.

The Patriote victory raised hopes. What dampened them was the news that their leader, Papineau, had fled. And though Nelson was competent as a military amateur, the rebels never really had a chance. The British beat them decisively at engagements in St. Charles and St. Eustache, and for the rest of his years, Nelson bitterly resented how Papineau snuck off to the United States while he spent months in a prison and was exiled later to Bermuda. Thanks to a legal loophole, Nelson managed to move to Plattsburg, New York, where he went back to practicing medicine.

An amnesty by the British government allowed Nelson to return to Montréal, where it was clear he had lost none of his revolutionary fire. He was elected to the first parliament and later served as Montréal's mayor. As mayor, he was one of the first to suggest making a public park on Mount Royal—today there is one. The former guest of the province's penitentiary system also served for a while as its inspector of jails and prisons.

Papineau had come home, too, and Nelson was determined to expose him as a coward and an autocrat. "It is perhaps a favour for which we should thank God that your projects failed, persuaded as I am at present that you would have governed with a rod of iron." While Nelson's record and integrity—if not his fierce temper—assured him a lasting place on the rolls of Québec's statesmen, Papineau's reputation was in ruins and his political comeback short-lived.

Nelson wasn't indiscriminate in his grudges. He actually wrote a letter once asking a British commander to help him dispel allegations of cruelty during the rebellion. He also has an interesting legacy beyond politics. He and his physician son were the first in Canada to operate using anesthetic. He also wrote a comprehensive bilingual pamphlet on preventing cholera.

Today in Québec, the annual paid holiday of National Patriotes Day is marked every year on the Monday before May 25—which is easy enough for the rest of Canada to remember since it's Victoria Day. When the holiday was introduced, it was recognized that Québecois didn't want to celebrate old ties to the British monarchy—ironically, they now help in part to mark the accomplishment of an Englishman working on their behalf.

Compared to the rebellion in the east, the one in Upper Canada was a pathetic, short-lived affair. William Lyon Mackenzie was no Wolfred Nelson, and while his grievances had merit, he was more bluster than bite. A recession was taking hold of the province after an especially bad harvest. All the British troops had been sent to Lower Canada where the insurrection was expected to be greatest. Mackenzie saw the moment to strike.

In a pamphlet issued in December 1837, he warned "a connection to England would involve us in all her wars," which was a convenient rewrite of history. In the last war, England was all that stopped American conquest. He called on supporters to gather at Montgomery's Tavern north of Toronto, his nominal headquarters. On December 5, he led a mob of rebels down Yonge Street.

Many of them were farmers and villagers tired from their night journey into town. Mackenzie had talked his hapless mob into thinking a show of force would be enough, and Toronto residents would flock to their sides. Instead, a small group of loyal militiamen waited to fire on them and shoot down his plan of establishing a provisional government.

What happened next was a skirmish, not a battle. Mackenzie, who never served in an army unit in his life, later blamed the rebellion's military commander, Samuel Lount, and his supporters, suggesting they "fell flat on their faces" after shooting, instead of moving off to the side for the next rank to fire. The simple country folk, he argued, assumed those in front were shot dead and so lost heart. The more likely reason is simpler. The men didn't run because they "imagined" men in front getting shot—they ran because *they* didn't want to get shot. They never expected resistance.

That was mostly it for the Upper Canada Rebellion. No glory at all. Two days later a larger force of militia blasted the rebels into tucking tail again and burned down Montgomery's Tavern. Lount was hanged, while Mackenzie escaped to Buffalo and became another exile in the United States. The rebellions in both Upper and Lower Canada sputtered on in 1838, with rebels launching attacks from the U.S. and Patriotes helped by sympathetic Americans. They were brutally suppressed, with Glengarry Highlanders set loose to pillage and burn and with more than 100 captured rebels shipped off to the Australian penal colony. The rebels did, however, alarm London into finally paying proper attention.

The British prime minister at the time was William Lamb, better known as the second and probably the most famous Lord Melbourne. A moderate pragmatist who had survived two sex scandals (Lord Byron had a fling with his wife), he mentored Queen Victoria in her early political education. About British North America, he couldn't have cared less. "The final separation of these colonies might possibly not be of material detriment to the interests of the mother-country," he wrote, "but it is clear that it would be a serious blow to the honour of Great Britain."

So for honour's sake, someone had to be sent to look in on these Canadians and maybe put some sense into their heads. Better to kill two birds with one stone by dispatching a certain someone who was intelligent and insightful, yet a constant pain in the ass for the government at home. Melbourne had in mind a fellow he personally disliked and was happy to send away on a long sea voyage.

Enter John George Lambton, the Earl of Durham. Durham had been an ambassador to Russia, a man who liked art and history and had refined tastes. Among the carriages and the packed uniforms and silver he had loaded onto ships sailing for Québec (all at his own expense), he also brought cases of dry champagne because he doubted the Canadian palate when it came to wine. He also has the strange distinction of having suffered the first case in Canada, treated by a Toronto doctor, of what's called synesthesia, a rare condition where the senses get mixed up (those with synesthesia, for instance, can associate numbers or letters with a certain colour).

Friends and enemies alike knew Durham as "Radical Jack." Radical, of course, was relative as the Victorian Age got underway. Descended from a family whose fortune was built in the coal mines of northern England, he was a champion of the middle classes rather than the poor. Durham supported the idea of a secret vote, which didn't exist in either Britain or Canada at the time, but he didn't want that vote available to everyone (and it wasn't). Durham had made himself a nuisance by actually suggesting Parliament needed reform.

He had no trouble handling his detractors. When a colleague informed him he couldn't side with him anymore because of his views, Durham's reply was a neat package of scathing wit. "I beg to say that I feel gratitude for your frankness, compassion for your fears, little dread of your opposition and no want of your support."

He stepped off a ship onto Québec soil armed with a healthy budget and sweeping authority to bring the colonies into line. He almost immediately dissolved the executive council and formed a new one with the staff that sailed over with him. Then he went on a whirlwind of inspections of the Canadas, scrutinizing their education systems and registry offices and meeting with officials. When he noticed Lower Canada had nothing better than a Town Watch, he modelled a new police service after London's own force developed by Robert Peel.

Durham also granted amnesty to a collection of the Lower Canada Patriotes and sent major rebels like Wolfred Nelson off to Bermuda. If his fellow politicians back in England thought he was being too lenient on the colonials, he pointed out in a letter to Queen Victoria that peace had been established without resorting to bloodshed: "The guilty have received justice, the misguided mercy; but at the same time, security is afforded to the loyal and peaceable subjects of this hitherto distracted province."

The problem was he had no right to send the exiles to Bermuda—it wasn't in his jurisdiction. Not that the governor of Bermuda complained or saw anything wrong with it. Melbourne, in fact, sent him a note of praise:

"I am very happy to hear that you have settled the very difficult affair of the prisoners and settled it so well."

But Melbourne and Durham's enemies soon seized on the issue of the colonial governor overstepping his authority. Durham didn't realize what a storm he'd caused until he read about it in a New York newspaper. Worse was the eventual discovery that Melbourne decided to sell him out in the House of Commons, changing his mind and countermanding Durham's ordinance over Bermuda.

He decided to quit. The papers in both Upper and Lower Canada were on his side, lambasting his fellow Whigs for their betrayal, and Durham's major critic in London was burned in effigy in the *Place d'Armes* in Québec City; Melbourne's Colonial Secretary was also depicted in effigy—fast asleep. Melbourne himself wrote to Durham, urging him to stay in Canada, but Radical Jack's mind was made up. He felt he "had no business here" anymore, and the military could mop up any further rebellion.

Durham's health had been poor during his brief tenure as governor. He had overworked himself and was exhausted. At midnight on Halloween, the night before his scheduled departure, he wrapped himself up in a large military cloak and went to the highest tower of Fort Saint-Louis to take a last look over Québec. Durham sailed back to London, but that wasn't the end of his influence on Canada.

He had spent less than five months in Lower Canada, and only three weeks in the rest of British North America. It was enough for him to push for sweeping recommendations, and in his townhouse on a little street near St. James Palace he finished his *Report on the Affairs of British North America*. In early 1839 he was ready to present it.

The report pushed for the basic ingredients of responsible government. No big surprise there, given his liberal sympathies, and Canadian advocates had been buttonholing him over this throughout his Canadian tour. Durham recommended a governor choose his councillors from members who had the elected confidence of the assembly. He also thought the best solution to all the bickering was to unite the two Canadas into one.

Interestingly, Durham may have had this idea before he ever set foot in Canada. While still at home, he made a point of calling on men who had visited the colonies already to get their advice. Granted, he could only solicit British points of view, but Radical Jack had a mind of his own and was determined to use it. One biographer suggests Durham might have been sold on the concept of revamping the Canadas along the federation model adopted by the United States. But Durham adjusted his opinion after he had direct experience of the country, and instead we've inherited the famous observation from his report:

"I expected to find a contest between a government and a people. I found two nations warring in the bosom of a single state: I found a struggle, not of principles, but of races; and I perceived that it would be idle to attempt any amelioration of laws or institutions until we could first succeed in terminating the deadly animosity that now separates the inhabitants of Lower Canada into the hostile divisions of French and English."

Opinions of the report have evolved with the ages. "The Durham Report has long been considered as the greatest state document in British Imperial history." So went the high praise written up by British historian Reginald Coupland. He breathlessly claimed its significance lay "in the fact that it established the principle on which the British Commonwealth of Nations has been built." Heady stuff, and it was all about Canada.

But Coupland, who himself was born in the waning years of the Victorian Age, was writing close to the half-way mark of the 20th century. There is no empire any-more. No one in England outside maybe a university campus would tilt their head at a reference to the report, and so it's up to us in Canada to weigh its importance.

Today's verdict is harsher in light of the report's analy-sis of the French situation. To Durham, the Canadiens had no history and no literature—a sweeping, ignorant statement that contradicts his contention of a struggle between races (if the Canadien culture didn't exist, there would be no struggle in the first place). No matter. Once the French were absorbed into the institutions and into a flourishing, single Anglo Canada, it would all work out.

"The language, the laws, the character of the North American Continent are English," argued Durham (who forgot entirely about Mexico), "and every race but English appears there in a condition of inferiority. It is to elevate them from that inferiority that I desire to give the Canadians our English character."

So we'll help you by slowly exterminating your own identity. Sounds like a plan.

The old apologists for Durham have pointed out he wasn't anti-French as such—his case was with the French institutions he believed were "calculated to repress the intelligence and freedom of the great mass of the people." A little over a century later, the Québecois were making the same accusation, directing them especially at the Roman Catholic Church. It was Durham's dismissal of culture and his solution that rankled.

There were French Canadians who were quite fluent in English and could read, and they argued they didn't need Durham's kind of help, thank you very much. There were protests over the idea of union. Meanwhile, François-Xavier Garneau—outraged by the report—got to work on his three-volume *Histoire du Canada*. So if it weren't for an Englishman's uninformed criticism, Francophones in Canada may have had to wait a little longer for their first comprehensive history.

Parliament in London naturally liked the idea of assimilation—the Canadas would be united. It was less enthusiastic about introducing responsible government, and Tories called Durham's report "disgraceful" and "mischievous." (You can't have people deciding things for themselves in a democracy! Where will it lead?) It would take years for the idea to take hold. When it finally did, it wasn't in either Canada at all, but in the Maritimes, and no violent rebellion was needed. All it took was a war of words.

In Nova Scotia, the same complaints were being grumbled over the behaviour of Her Majesty's Council, the same lack of representation, and there was no mitigating issue of language. You only had to follow the money.

In 1825, privateer Enos Collins, who did so well in the War of 1812 buying captured American vessels, made what you might call a lateral career move into banking. He and his chums set up the Halifax Banking Company. No problem worrying about regulations or political oversight—five of his business partners sat on the council. The rest of the 12-member council were friends and relatives of Collins or his pals. By 1833, the bank directors and council members made a mess out of handling a second incorporated bank, which should have been predictable since it was a mere puppet of the monopoly. The province's currency depreciated, and as the classic Halifax historian Thomas Raddall put it, "The situation stank in the nostrils of all but the successive military governors."

One man, however, was sick of the smell coming from the ironstone bank building on Water Street. This was Joseph Howe, and we have to count ourselves lucky his older brother got to take over the family business. Their father was a United Empire Loyalist who fled Massachusetts and became Nova Scotia's postmaster general and the king's printer. Young Joseph had to find work elsewhere.

He knew printing and he was bookish, so he turned to journalism and soon became the sole owner of *The Novascotian*. Like any good journalist, Howe had an insatiable curiosity for current events everywhere, and he had a publisher's necessary fearlessness. He also had just the right measure of oddball in his character. On summer nights, he would walk down George Street to the edge of the harbour, strip down and throw himself into the Atlantic.

The provincial assembly wrangled and debated amendments, threw out others, but the second bank—what would grow up in time to be Scotiabank—was still the council's creature. And the council held the real power. Fed up, Howe published in 1835 an excoriating attack on the powers-that-be in the form of an anonymous letter, claiming they had "by one stratagem or other, taken from the pockets of the people, in over exactions, fines, etc., etc., a sum that would exceed in the gross amount £30,000."

This, boys and girls, was then and still is now a textbook case of libel. Lawyers told Howe he didn't have a prayer and they wouldn't take the case, so he ended up defending himself in court. Now be glad that there is one English tradition we've somehow not inherited. In England, if I sue you for libel, the onus is actually on *you* to prove you didn't do it.

(This precedent is still alive and well in our modern day. In 1996, for instance, *The Guardian* faced financial ruin when British Tory politician Neil Hamilton sued it over the cash-for-questions-in-Parliament scandal. Even though what the paper printed was fact, it incredibly could still have lost on legal grounds. But at the 11th hour, disgusted government MPs sank Hamilton themselves by turning incriminating documents over to the paper. *The Guardian* chronicled the whole thing with the blazing, bold headline: "A LIAR AND A CHEAT." Hamilton withdrew his suit, slunk away in shame and now seems to make a career out of appearing on chat shows.)

The law was different then, enough so that Howe couldn't even debate the particulars of the accusations in open court. He had one thing going for him in his libel case—a jury trial. He used more rhetoric than reason to plead his case, pointing out his accusers had done nothing to clear their name through a transparent inquiry. Then he took a nasty swipe at his enemies, claiming he didn't write the anonymous letter, because after all, "I had satisfied myself, and if the opportunity were afforded, I would satisfy you, that by the neglect, incompetence and corruption of the parties charged, we have been annually despoiled of a much larger amount."

Nice logic: I didn't say you stole, because if I did, I would have said you stole *more*.

Amazingly, he won.

Encouraged by his victory, Howe went into politics and was elected to the provincial assembly. It didn't take long for him to be frustrated by its lack of power. Unlike Papineau, Nelson and Mackenzie, however, Howe only sought reform. The idea of violent insurrection was unthinkable to him. "I wish to live and die a British subject—but not a Briton only in name."

As an elected official, he still got into trouble. After publishing an inflammatory article in 1840 about rich children, the son of the chief justice, John Haliburton, challenged him to a duel. On an early Saturday morning, Haliburton shot first and missed. Howe, who was a decent shot, decided to fire in the air to teach "a lesson of coolness and moderation."

Howe was never a believer in party politics, but used his various offices to thump away for responsible government. Here, too, sentiment was growing for Nova Scotia to decide more of its fate (in 1834, the British government thought nothing of dumping a group of outpatients infected with cholera from Chelsea Hospital into Halifax). When Durham tabled his report, Howe lobbied for its recommendations, despite wanting Nova Scotia to have nothing to do with the Canadas.

It took about 10 years, but in late January 1848, after the old Tory guard lost a no-confidence motion, the Reform party—which eventually accepted Howe as its leader—was elected and formed the first responsible government in Canada. It was, in fact, the first responsible government in the whole British Empire.

There was no turning back the tide. By May, New Brunswick had elected its own responsible government, and Prince Edward Island and Newfoundland followed a few years later.

In 1849, an ugly, violent spectacle in Québec was the postscript to the Rebellions. One of Durham's recommendations was to compensate those in Lower Canada who suffered property damage from the insurrection. From the Tory point of view in the region, this was like saying, "Here, have some cash for taking up arms against our country." The Tories thought many Patriotes were still lurking around, having gotten away with treason. And they considered the Rebellion Losses Bill an outrage, a sellout.

The new governor general, Lord Elgin, accepted the passage of the bill, since this is what governors general do in responsible government. (Maybe it helped that Elgin was Durham's son-in-law.) When he rode away from the assembly building, a mob pelted his carriage with eggs.

The protesters weren't done. That night, a mob vented its full fury on Montréal's assembly building. Some thug jumped into the Speaker's chair and "dissolved" parliament, while someone else carried off the ceremonial mace, and the building was set on fire—the gas lighting that had been installed made it easier to burn. Assembly members scrambled out to safety while precious historical documents and decorative paintings all burned. A clergyman who saw the riot echoed Durham's assessment in calling the feud "a war of races—English speaking people will not be ruled by a Canadian government, and none can see what the end of these things will yet be...."

Anyone who wants to know why beautiful Montréal is not the capital of Canada or even of Québec—well, blame the English. If Montréal's Anglo citizens hadn't gone on a rampage, maybe things would be different. Discretion being the better part of valour, the capital of the new Province of Canada was moved for a while to Toronto, where there was far less chance of any French–English spats blowing up into another riot (the capital shifted back and forth between Toronto and Québec City until just before Confederation).

Despite the bloodshed and the bitter grudges that followed the Rebellions, something unique had been achieved, another first for the colony that so often exasperated the English in London and was relegated to an afterthought. British North America was inexorably evolving toward a new political destiny. But it was far from finished yet with its English roots.

THE BLUE AND THE GREY AND THE BLUE AND THE RED AND THE WHITE

Warning: This is not a chapter about Confederation. I know you covered all that in school, and I wouldn't *dream* of subjecting you to a tired rehash of our hallowed Fathers of Confederation and our drunken Scotsman of a prime minister who never liked this place anyway (and he certainly didn't like Englishmen). Besides, there's the little matter of the American Civil War that came first, and if it hadn't been for Americans *still* wanting to get hold of us while the English claimed to be disinterested but were *still* occasionally mucking about in U.S. business, maybe we wouldn't have a larger, more united country in the first place, because there were repercussions for us even beyond Confederation…

Or didn't you know?

Toronto served as a kind of Civil War-era version of *Casablanca*, but instead of "Rick's," everybody came to the Queen's Hotel (torn down in 1928 to be replaced by the Royal York). Confederate spies visited neutral Canada to plot raids on northern states. John Wilkes Booth sat down with conspirators in Montréal's St. Lawrence Hall Hotel to plot the assassination of Lincoln. That particular hotel saw so many Confederates the hotel management made a point of making them feel right at home by offering mint juleps. In fact, when it was thought Booth hadn't been shot and had actually escaped, Montréal detectives conducted a massive search for the assassin.

Strangely, none of this was enough provocation for the United States to turn again on Canada—not that they required much. Lincoln's Machiavellian Secretary of State, William H. Seward, thought it would be a brilliant distraction from America's internal squabble if Canada was invaded and annexed. That would mean waging war on Britain, which suited him just fine. Seward was a rabid Anglophobe who once joked to a duke that if he ever became Secretary of State, he would consider it "my duty to insult England, and I mean to do so."

Great Britain was in a difficult position over the American Civil War. Queen Victoria declared Britain neutral one day after the outbreak of hostilities, but that meant a tacit recognition of the Confederacy as an equal player. Not that there wasn't sympathy for the South in Britain—the textile industry depended on Southern cotton. But the Confederates who crossed the ocean and turned up on their doorstep annoyed the British—especially when one of them, James Murray Mason of Virginia, had the distasteful habit of chewing tobacco while visiting the British Parliament and missing the spitoon. Another, John Slidell of Louisiana, had limited diplomatic experience and reputedly alienated his Confederate colleagues overseas by being a drunk.

In November 1861, Mason and Slidell were onboard the British mail steamer, *Trent*, which had left port in Havana on its way to London. But Captain Charles Wilkes, a loyal defender of the Union, made it his personal mission to go after them. Wilkes was a famed Antarctic explorer, a circumnavigator of the globe and an unrepentant loose cannon. He had already been court-martialled over an episode of disobeying orders and insulting the Navy secretary, earning himself a three-year suspension.

In 1861, Wilkes had simple orders: take command of the warship *San Jacinto* off Africa's west coast and sail it back to Philadelphia. But when he got a tip about the Confederate envoys, he sent his ship into the Bahama Channel after the *Trent*. A few of Wilkes' officers protested the idea of detaining a British vessel in neutral waters—the captain had them arrested.

In capturing the diplomats, Wilkes became the hero of the hour in the North, with Congress voting to award him a special gold medal. The British wanted his head. Prime Minister Palmerston informed his cabinet: "You may stand for this, but damned if I will." The *Times* of London fumed about American vulgarity and cowardice, while the government demanded Slidell and Mason be released, and oh, a formal apology to Britain while you're at it.

As war loomed again, everyone knew where the battle-field would be—that's right, you're on it. Here, Canada: a replay of 1812. Mobs demonstrated outside the house of the U.S. consul in Halifax. The governor general, Lord Monck, ordered the military commander for British North America to beef up the militias. Meanwhile,

11,000 British troops were sent over to reinforce defences.

The United States was already at war—with itself. Politicians in the North were almost suicidally gunning to take on Britain, even though the defeats at Fort Sumter and the first Battle of Bull Run should have told them something about the quality of their commanders. Congress spent $750,000 to shore up fortifications at key spots like Buffalo and Detroit. But Lincoln was president, and he fortunately had a cooler head—and a memory. "We fought Great Britain in 1812 for doing just what Captain Wilkes has done," he pointed out. "We must give up the prisoners and apologize."

This did not go down well with his Secretary of State; Lincoln recalled he was "loaded to the muzzle" with arguments against England. Too bad. The president considered the Confederate diplomats "white elephants," and they were freed on Christmas Day. It must have just killed Seward to have to draft up the necessary document to send off to London, and he used some weaselly rationalizations so the U.S. government could save face. There were sighs of relief along the border with Canada, and Lincoln turned his attention back to those maddening commanders who refused to take the initiative and clobber the South quick and hard. The idea of invading Canada and fighting Britain faded.

Of course, there had been those who never wanted to pay attention to history. At the height of the *Trent* Affair, *The New York Herald* bragged that the U.S. could pour 150,000 troops into the Province of Canada and take it over in three weeks. It also claimed two-thirds of the province would love to join the Union. Since in living memory of older citizens, British soldiers had set fire to Washington, hopefully there was a 19th-century equivalent to Rick Mercer pacing around Toronto or Halifax, pointing out how it would be tougher than they thought.

Or maybe it wouldn't be. By now Britain had the largest empire in history, but London was tired of the cost and the effort of defending a sizable chunk of it. The London *Spectator* grumbled it wasn't the duty of those at home "to defend men who will not defend themselves."

Now this is interesting. No one ever suggested pulling troops out of India or British possessions in Africa, but in these places Britain was an occupying power. Those in London saw Canadians (apart from the French kind) as provincial versions of themselves: white, English, oh, less sophisticated, *of course*—but still, why couldn't these people handle their own defences?

This Canada and the eastern seaboard holdings seemed hardly worth the bother at times. And in fact, Britain did more trade with the United States than with its own North American colonies. It would be this way until two decades into the 20th century.

Despite Lord Monck using all his diplomatic skill to win friends and influence people for a Militia Bill in 1862, it failed to win passage in the Canadian legislature. Raising and maintaining militia troops was sure to be an expensive enterprise. Why couldn't Britain defend Canada? Wasn't that part of the job description for those in London who were supposed to be running the empire?

As soon as the flap died down over the *Trent*, the British troops who had sailed over promptly went home. Sir John A. Macdonald correctly pointed out that "had war come on, as it unquestionably would but for the fortunate termination of the *Trent* difficulty, we should have been utterly unprepared to meet the foe." The Militia

Bill died in part because Macdonald was deep in the bottle at the time, but when he was lucid, he was formulating a new vision.

During the four long years when the United States came close to self-destruction, he watched and studied. He was convinced the fissure that cracked open and split the American Union could be traced back to a weak federal government. He wanted to make sure any new Canadian political entity avoided this trap, while a new consolidation of the provinces helped safeguard against American encroachment.

It was true there had been an evolution toward the idea of the provinces coming together. The Maritimes certainly wanted to unify and recognized the economic benefits. There were those hammering away for representation by population: "Rep by Pop." Still, if Mother England had showed a little more interest in defending British North America, there wouldn't have been such a surge of momentum to get the whole thing finally *done*.

Another political mess from the Civil War that involved England might have added an additional push. Strangely enough, it involved another ship—but this time the issue wasn't boarding, it was building.

The ship in question was the *Alabama*. It was the most successful of the Confederate ships to run the Union blockade, having sailed from the Pacific Rim to South America and capturing or sinking 65 Northern merchant vessels. What also galled the Union was, as *Harper's Magazine* pointed out, "She was to all intents a British vessel, built at a British dock…." The *Alabama*'s surgeon onboard was British, and after the war, two of the ship's officers moved to Nova Scotia and became members of the business community.

As 1862 was drawing to a close, William Seward could do nothing about the *Alabama* running rings around Union ships, but he could vent his outrage on its manufacturers. The United States expected London to pay for damages inflicted by British-built Confederacy vessels on the North. London filed counter-claims over Union ship damage to British vessels. And the British had one irrefutable argument that blew holes in the American case—the Union didn't seem to have any problem with the British building *their* ships!

Newspapers in Canada hammered away in editorials about the contradictory, hypocritical behaviour on the part of the North. The *Hamilton Spectator* demanded, "Now, we would like to know what difference there is between Confederates buying ships in Britain for war purposes, and the Federals purchasing horses in Canada for the use of their cavalry?" It wasn't a case of buying any old nag; another paper learned a Union agent had spent about $20,000 on horses in Ingersoll.

In June 1864, the *U.S.S. Kearsarge* opened fire on the *Alabama* in (and this didn't help) the English Channel off Cherbourg, France. After an hour-long battle, the *Kearsarge* sank the naval pride of the Confederacy. But the Americans wouldn't let the issue die. They still wanted compensation.

The chairman of the U.S. Senate Foreign Relations Committee, Charles Sumner, was insisting by 1869 that Britain cough up more than two billion dollars in "indirect claims," and it could pay off part of its tab by handing over Canada. As you can imagine, William Seward—still Secretary of State under Andrew Johnson—loved this idea. He was open to taking British Columbia, the British Caribbean holdings or all of British North America. Britain declined.

What had now become known as the Alabama Claims ended up going to international arbitration in 1872 under provisos of the new Treaty of Washington between the U.S. and Britain. The arbitration board threw out the American charge that Britain was responsible for prolonging the war. But the U.S. did get to leave the table with something: $15.5 million in "private" damages and Britain's formal expression of regret (not quite an apology but in the ballpark).

Obviously, the U.S. did *not* get Canada. We're still here. But interestingly, the arbitration board wasn't done with its work yet, and it decided many things that are part of the makeup of our modern nation. For one, a ruling on who owned the San Juan Islands off the West Coast—a holdover issue from the War of 1812—was given to Kaiser Wilhelm of Germany, who decided America should have them. Worse news was that the Maritimes lost lucrative inshore fishing rights for about a decade under the Treaty.

But the arbitration board also decided the Great Lakes would be shared by both the U.S. and Canada—and that included Lake Michigan which sits completely in American geography. Canada also got the Yukon. So because Englishmen in Liverpool shipyards were building sloops-of-war for the Confederate army, Canadians were able 30 years later to rush off in droves to Dawson City for the Klondike Gold Rush. Even indirectly, the English were helping create Canada.

One of the oddest tales of how the American Civil War affected Canada concerns an Englishman unknown to most Canadians. But then anonymity is a good thing for a spy.

In 1865, the U.S. Civil War was over, but relations between America and Canada stayed complicated thanks to a group of fanatical loons, the Fenians. The Fenians were Irish immigrants to the United States, and you can see why they held a bitter grudge toward England. Things hadn't improved much for Ireland since the time of Cromwell, and the British government ignored millions dying during the Great Famine in the 1840s as it kept exporting corn from Ireland. The Irish had a whole stack of bones to pick with the English over language, land, education, suffrage and civil rights.

According to the Fenians' convoluted logic, however, the best way to free Ireland from British imperial domination was to come up north out of the United States to attack Canada. It does make the head spin.

They were terrorists. The good news was that they were mostly incompetent terrorists. In raid after Fenian raid, the Canadian militia easily booted them back across the border. Like all terrorists, however, they inspired fear. When the Fenians tried hitting Upper Canada, John A. Macdonald suspended habeas corpus for any suspected members of their group. Rumours were rife of an invasion in New Brunswick (the Fenians' first step was to allegedly take over Campobello Island), and that made great political fodder for Samuel Tilley and other pro-Confederation Liberals to win an already rigged, ballot-stuffed election.

When the American Civil War started, a young man in Colchester named Thomas Beach wasn't thinking of Ireland at all but how he could find adventure in the United States. Still in his teens, he'd escaped a dreary career as a draper's assistant to head to London and then

Paris. He must have been inspired in part by his brothers, one who fought against the Zulus in South Africa and another who served with General Garnet Wolseley—not in Western Canada, but when Wolseley put down an insurrection in Egypt.

Beach managed to find his way to the States to enlist in the Union Army, and still floating on a daydream of European romanticism, he took the alias, Henri Le Caron, a name he borrowed from a restaurant family in Paris. Beach rose from being a bugler in Nashville to a lieutenant still in his early twenties, and when he heard about incidents of Fenianism, he wrote home about it to his father—who promptly wrote to the British Foreign Secretary.

When the Civil War was over and Beach came home for a family visit, Irish terrorism both in Canada and in England was a priority at the Home Office. With London undergoing one of its first (but certainly not its last) bomb panics, Beach sat in a Harley Street townhouse, weighing the invitation from British officials to become a spy. He was to become successful beyond anyone's imagination.

Less than a year after returning to America, he sat in the Oval Office, now as Major Henri Le Caron, listening to President Andrew Johnson apologize for not doing more to help the Irish Revolutionaries take over Canada during the war. Beach was still writing to his father about his activities, confiding in February 1868,

> Canada is as I told you before their field of coming action, and Andy Johnson's administration will not impede their progress a great deal. He said only a few days ago…'I have always sympathized with this movement but a man can't always do officially what he feels unofficially….'

135

Beach made himself indispensable, warning the British and Canadian governments about a plot to assassinate the Prince of Wales and keeping them apprised of Fenian arms shipments. He was so well trusted that he was elevated to the rank of major in the Irish Republican Army, entrusted with consolidating different revolutionary groups in the eastern U.S. He was tickled that he was paid handsome salaries by both sides to conspire against each other, though he reserved a bigoted contempt for the Irish as a "pack of low, dirty foul mouthed beings."

It wasn't such a joke though when he was recognized as a Fenian during a train stop in Cornwall, Ontario, and an impromptu lynch mob shouted, "Hang him!" He saved his life only by confiding in the town's mayor and pleading to be sent on to Ottawa under guard so that his identity could be verified. In the capital, the checks were made and his bravado returned, and he celebrated with anti-Fenians at a private club, laughing over how I.R.A. actually stood for "I Ran Away."

England had given Canada one of its most successful spies, and it was English affairs that took him away. In 1887, the Irish Protestant MP Charles Stewart Parnell, one of the champions for Ireland's Home Rule, was implicated in republican violence by a series of forged letters published in the London *Times*. A commission of inquiry was set up, and Parnell hoped, as it got rolling the next year, that it would be restricted to just the authenticity of the letters. But it became a probe into Irish revolutionary violence, one that carried the danger of ruining his reputation, especially given his public attitudes and his private conversations endorsing militant activities—including one talk with "Henri Le Caron."

It was time for Beach to out himself. He claimed he wanted people to know the extent of the danger of the

Irish rebel groups, but he also had more personal motives for going public. Never very good with money, he negotiated with the *Times* for his witness testimony. By now, he and his family lived in Chicago, and his wife packed in such a hurry for escape back to England that she left behind incriminating letters to Beach's spymaster in London, Robert Anderson, who was about to become the head of Scotland Yard.

On the stand in the Royal Courts of Justice, Beach testified that Parnell believed in insurrection to win Ireland its freedom. Parnell's lawyer did his best with his cross-examination to rattle Beach, but the double agent stuck to his story. Meanwhile, British intelligence agents moved Beach's family in case they were attacked.

The lawyer did better when he went after the real author of the letters, a journalist who broke under pressure on the witness stand and who fled to Madrid, where he shot himself in the head in a hotel room. The inquiry went on, but as one reporter put it, it was now "a funeral of dead reputations." Parnell went back to Parliament, vindicated, and Beach slipped away to live a quiet life, still in the pay of the British Secret Service and always looking over his shoulder. He confounded the Irish revolutionaries he betrayed, dying quietly at home in South Kensington in London.

Beach's crusade, arguably his feud and his grudge, was with Irish republican militancy and nationalism. As with all spies, the political landscape that was behind his work was an ephemeral one. Ireland would eventually be partitioned, and a republic would be born. Whatever his motivations, Thomas Beach's labours in secret helped prevent a threat of terrorism in our country and provided another impetus for the provinces to unite in

Confederation. An Englishman hardly anyone knows helped bring the country together.

I promised this wasn't a chapter on Confederation, and it still isn't, not really, but we can't neglect the fact that England played its part—at least as a backdrop and for the final signoff to send us on our way. Canada became a national entity right in the heart of London.

In fact, many Canadian tourists may not realize it, but when they go over to the British capital and see the main tourist sites, they're probably stepping in the footsteps of Macdonald and the others. How? Well, if you go to where Victoria Street intersects with Tothill Street and stand back to get a look at Westminster Abbey, you'll have good odds of being right on the spot where our first prime minister likely walked.

Macdonald and the others stayed at the Westminster Palace Hotel, which alas, no longer exists. What stands there now at that address, not far from the British Parliament, is a post-Art Deco office block, one that's retained the hotel's original wedge shape. Granted, there's not much to see here as a legacy of Canadian history, but if it's your first time in London, you were going to see Westminster Abbey anyway, weren't you?

It was at this hotel that we nearly lost Macdonald. He was exhausted one evening in his room and fell asleep while reading newspapers by candlelight. He woke up to discover his bedclothes, his sheets and the room's curtains on fire. Frantically, he tore down the curtains, emptied a water jug on them and then ripped open a bolster and pillows to dump "an avalanche of feathers on the blazing mess." Then he rushed next door for help to the rooms of George Étienne Cartier and Alexander Galt of Québec. Macdonald realized a few minutes later he'd been burned on his hands, shoulder blade and forehead, but he recovered and considered his escape miraculous.

It was in London where the Fathers of Confederation hammered out the final deal, and Macdonald rightly deserves the bulk of the credit. He drafted most of the resolutions for the British North America Act, and for a conference on creating the political design of a new political entity, he was the only one there with a background in constitutional law.

Joseph Howe was also in London, trying to stop Confederation in its tracks. He believed in Nova Scotia and was still all for maintaining British ties—just not with Canada. "I am a dear lover of old England," he declared, "and to save her would blow Nova Scotia into the air or scuttle her like an old ship." Being one for sea metaphors, Howe was opposed to the "catamaran of a Confederacy."

It was 1867, and with the *Alabama* affair still in the news, Howe made the argument to British politicians that the country west of Québec simply couldn't be defended, not without an inter-colonial railroad. Britain, on the other hand, was still quite capable of defending the Maritimes; it shouldn't injure Nova Scotia's loyalty by undermining its self-contained responsible government. Howe had come to London with a petition of 30,000 signatures against union with Canada. He even managed to get a few London papers on his side.

But Howe came up against the stone wall of the latest colonial secretary, Henry Herbert, the Earl of Carnarvon, who believed in Macdonald's vision of a united Canada. "We are laying the foundation of a great State," Carnarvon told Parliament, "perhaps one which at a future day may even overshadow this country. But, come what may, we shall rejoice that we have shown neither indifference to their wishes nor jealousy of their aspirations, but that we honestly and sincerely, to the utmost of our power and knowledge, fostered their growth, recognizing in it the conditions of our own greatness."

The bill made its tedious way through readings, but it was racing against time. British MPs wanted to delay its passage until they could figure out the annoying issue of the Reform Bill being pushed by Benjamin Disraeli and the prime minister, Lord Derby. No Conservatives wanted to bother with Canada when (shock, horror!) there were men in the House who wanted to give the vote to the working classes of England. Carnarvon was one of the cabinet members who couldn't stomach the Reform Bill, but he was eager to see the British North America Act passed. John A. Macdonald was stuck with watching and waiting, hoping it went through.

Joseph Howe felt just as powerless in the visitors gallery of the Commons, frustrated that "country gentlemen who could not maybe point out Nova Scotia on the map" were more interested in a bill over fox hounds than colonial affairs. He confessed he wasn't "prepared for the utter indifference, and manifest disposition to get rid of us." In time, of course, Howe gave up the fight and accepted Nova Scotia as part of the Canadian fold, but he had a long, bitter sail home to Halifax in defeat.

On the day the bill passed through committee in the British House of Commons, Carnarvon announced he was quitting as Colonial Secretary over Reform. But by now his work was done and Canada's unified future was safe. There wasn't even any debate when the bill passed its third reading. Queen Victoria signed the bill for the British North America Act on March 29, 1867.

The new political entity would have a unique name as well. Before Carnarvon had resigned, he had explained to Victoria, "The North American delegates are anxious that the United Provinces should be designated as the 'Dominion of Canada.' It is a new title: but intended on their part as a tribute to the monarchical principle which they earnestly desire to uphold."

As Canada was born, its official status still implied its ties to Mother England. Englishmen, in fact, were coming from across the Atlantic to help the country expand all the way to another ocean.

THE LAST, BEST WEST

I t doesn't get said enough: the Canadian Prairies are beautiful. They are also peculiar. It's possible, just possible, to fool yourself for a while that you're actually in the American Midwest. There are plenty of small towns where country music plays and where grain elevators with chipped paint rise above the relentlessly flat landscape. Then as you drive your way into Dauphin, Manitoba, or certain locales across the Prairies, you suddenly spot the onion dome of an Eastern Orthodox Church. What is *that* doing there?

Then there's the anachronism of language in Manitoba. Working off and on in broadcasting over the years, I still run into announcers in Ontario who want to pronounce the name Portage La Prairie with a French accent. "If you do that," I warn them, "you'll hear laughter all the way from Alberta." But it's French, they insist. Yes, so what?

Patiently, you try to explain there hasn't been anyone to pronounce it "*Por-taaahge La Prair-eee*" in generations.

Why are the Prairies so peculiar? The English have something to do with it. Our first prime minister wasn't terribly interested in the region, but with his cantankerous Scottish practicality, he admitted, "I would be quite willing to leave that whole country a wilderness for the next half century, but I fear that if Englishmen do not go there, Yankees will."

Englishmen did go there, but as it happened, not enough of them. Others, however, would do just as well.

Before we explore that, however, we have to check in on how the Hudson's Bay Company (HBC) was doing all that time, and you'll see why you were warned earlier against any patriotic grief over the corporation being bought up by Americans. By the Confederation era, the HBC was an organization that might as well have been a country unto itself—if you'd like a country that's run by the Mafia.

Its clerks ridiculously overcharged for goods, knowing they ran a monopoly. They thought nothing of invading the homes of Red River colonists—with the obliging help of police—to confiscate goods they claimed were sold illegally. Traders plied Natives with rum for their transactions. The Company could rig trials and did. It bribed officials. Though you might think of the HBC as a Canadian institution, that's a modern sentiment—it had absolutely no allegiance to Britain or Canada. Its ruthless administrator, George Simpson, told a whopping, bald-faced lie in 1857 to a parliamentary investigation: "I do not think that any part of the Hudson's Bay territories is well adapted for settlement; the crops are very uncertain."

Thankfully, his word for this wasn't good enough, and the British government dispatched Captain John Palliser to explore the HBC lands. With Confederation and the U.S. purchase of Alaska, there was increasing pressure on the Company to sell its property. It would have happily sold out to the Americans, but London wouldn't allow this. The Company answered that, sure, it could hand its territory over to the Crown—that will be £1,000,000 in cash, please.

One man wasn't buying. In 1858—about a decade before Carnarvon was helping Macdonald unify Canada—the colonial secretary was Edward Bulwer Lytton. Lytton is remembered today less for his political career than for his dubious reputation as a novelist. He's the one who gave us *The Last Days of Pompeii* and such literary gems as "the pen is mightier than the sword" and the infamously terrible opening line that goes "It was a dark and stormy night."

Lytton was an imperialist, but one who could see shades of grey in the Union Jack. In one of his books, *My Novel* (yes, he got away with naming it that), he mentioned "the empire on which the sun never sets. Poor Sun, how tired he must be—but not more tired than the Government." He backed the introduction of colonial self-government and looked forward to Canada achieving "safe and gradual independence which should be the last crowning boon that a colony should receive from a parent state."

He had his doubts about the British in India, thinking the East India Company might perhaps do a better job than London in handling the bad blood between Muslims and Hindus, but he recognized the abuses of the Hudson's Bay Company. Lytton took a particular interest in British Columbia and gave James Douglas an ultimatum:

he could be governor of Vancouver Island or he could be a high-ranking official for the Hudson's Bay Company, but he couldn't be both. It's ironic that Douglas gave up the HBC and wound up with more power as governor of an island attached to the mainland colony.

It's generally acknowledged that Lytton had sincere if typically paternalistic concern for the Native peoples. No doubt hearing early reports of how the region was wild with booze and violence, he told the British Commons that the Natives of British Columbia had to be safeguarded "from terrible demoralization."

One of the first who envisioned a colonial province of British Columbia, he assigned a detachment of Royal Engineers to go take a look at the terrain (the town of Lytton, where the Fraser and Thompson Rivers meet, is named after him). In a speech sending them off, he instructed them, "You will carefully refrain from quarrel or brawl. You will scorn, I am sure, the vice that degrades God's rational creature to that level of the brute—I mean the vice of intoxication…. You are not common soldiers—you are to be the Pioneers of Civilization."

It's clear Lytton didn't know many engineers.

As for the Hudson's Bay Company, the writing was on the wall over its vast holdings, and it was no longer a question of *if* the land would go to the Crown as when and how. As the Company played for time and demanded a high price, Lytton curtly told its management he'd rescind its trading rights unless it verified its charter with the Privy Council—which could very well say no. Luckily for the HBC, Lord Palmerston got back into power and appointed a new colonial secretary, the latest Duke of Newcastle.

That didn't let the HBC off the hook. The pressure was still mounting. A former manager of the Manchester, Sheffield and Lincolnshire Railway, Edward Watkin, thought a railway should cut right through Rupert's Land to connect the Atlantic to the Pacific. Newcastle talked the idea over with the latest HBC governor, Henry Barens, who once sat on the board of the Bank of England. Barens was horrified, but once he calmed down, he agreed the HBC would have to throw in the towel and sell its property. Newcastle asked him on the spot to offer a figure. Barens gave one, and that was that. Our country mushroomed in size because the Old Boys' Network from the "City"—the business district of London—haggled a price in a few minutes. By October 1868, a Canadian delegation was back at the Westminster Palace Hotel in London. The Duke of Newcastle presided over the finishing touches on a deal that paid the Company £1.5 million for a quarter of the North American continent.

Since it was necessary for us to discuss the Hudson's Bay Company and Lytton, and Lytton was so keen on British Columbia, we might as well finish with how BC joined Canada, which happened before the great changes on the Prairies anyway. Throughout all this time, one man had been pushing and pushing British Columbia's case—first, to be united with Vancouver Island and then to join the Confederation fold. His role suggests BC was the land of eccentrics from the beginning. Granted, the man we're talking about was an import.

This man was William Smith, whose name sounds dull, and it must have sounded that way to its owner because he legally changed it in 1854 to Amor de Cosmos. He was the son of United Empire Loyalists in Nova Scotia, but he left his native province in his late twenties for the gold fields of California. After finding his way up to

British Columbia, he fell into journalism (it's interesting how many of our statesmen were in this field) and founded *The British Colonist.*

De Cosmos was a huge admirer of Joseph Howe, and his views and his life paralleled Howe's in many respects. Like Howe, he was a devout Anglophile: "In Confederated Britain, Canada should take a position second only to England itself." But he was a complicated individual in his own right with erratic attitudes, his own special socialist sympathies (even though he sank his money into real estate and investments, some of which were highly speculative), a hate for the Hudson's Bay Company and a personal loathing for James Douglas.

Making his way around Victoria in his top hat and frock coat while carrying a big-handled walking stick (which he didn't always use for walking), he alienated many with his egotism and what they considered a condescending manner.

Community next to the Fort Victoria fur trading post, Vancouver Island. Photograph by the British Northwest Boundary Survey, 1858–1861.

Also like his hero, Joseph Howe, de Cosmos turned from journalism to politics, eventually becoming BC's second premier and later a federal MP. He worked hard for inclusion in Canada and met with Macdonald, who decided he'd much rather deal with another British Columbia representative who was…well, less colourful. In some ways, de Cosmos was ahead of his time. He envisioned an imperial parliament where the colonies elected members and Canada enjoyed "the appointment of the Governor General from among our people," instead of us just getting the person London chose.

British Columbia joined Canada in 1871, but its Father of Confederation came to a bad end. De Cosmos exhibited more and more bizarre behaviour in his last years. In 1879, he moved a resolution (which nobody dreamed of seconding) that BC opt out of Canada, and then in 1882, he wanted Canada to split away from the Empire. He lost his riding; he was already losing friends and supporters. He began wandering the streets of Victoria, getting into fights, shouting gibberish at strangers, until he was declared out of his mind and put away until he died.

So the English connection made its way down from the Loyalists to Joseph Howe, who inspired Amor de Cosmos, who brought British Columbia into Canada. De Cosmos also began an informal and unusual tradition of British Columbia electing eccentric leaders, from a premier who buys submarines to one who lived in a Dutch-themed fantasy castle.

The Hudson's Bay Company surrendering its land, of course, didn't make Western Canada English. Before Manitoba joined Confederation in 1870, it went through the crucible of the Métis Rebellion led by Louis Riel, and there are pockets of Francophones on the Prairies to this day, as well as First Nations people and Métis. The conversion of the West into an Anglo enclave was largely the work of Manitoba politician Clifford Sifton, who became the federal Minister of Interior for Wilfrid Laurier's government around the end of the 19th century.

Sifton hatched a scheme of generous land offers and an over-the-top sales job to fill up the Prairies with new settlers. Under the Dominion Lands Act, new arrivals could get 65 hectares of land for virtually a song. All it took was a ten-dollar registration fee. Meanwhile, Sifton sent agents to Britain, the U.S. and Europe to spread the glowing word about the fabulous land. There were lecture tours and about a million pamphlets distributed, with promotional lies that would make P.T. Barnum proud: "The frontier of Manitoba is about the same latitude as Paris."

Many of the new immigrants were English, but the Canadian Prairies must have been a culture shock, especially after Sifton's hype. England is a land where Nature isn't politely tamed—it's beaten into submission. The countryside is often a spectacularly "green and pleasant land" as Shakespeare promised, its gardens neat and tidy, and you can figure out where Sherwood Forest ends. In Canada, the English arrivals faced vast stretches of unending wilderness, with some winters when skin froze on contact with the air in under two minutes and soil on the Prairies that's specific in what it will grow. Some went home, disillusioned. Others resettled in the evolving towns.

In fact, it can't be coincidence that the English seemed to leave their mark most on the urban communities rather than the rural settings. Sifton would have preferred British settlers, but decided not to be picky and widened his net. He looked to Eastern Europeans. It says something about the resilient character of the Ukrainians and the Icelanders, the Poles and the Finns who accepted his invitation—not that they came, but that they *stayed*. An Eastern Orthodox Ukrainian or a Doukhobor from Russia could make an easier adjustment to the climate and often the landscape than, say, an English coalminer who fled the damp and mild temperatures of Tunbridge Wells, Kent.

Even with the multicultural feel of the Prairies, the region was still firmly English in sentiment. Sometimes this lapsed into self-parody, the phenomenon you see of other immigrant peoples when they become more Greek than the Greeks of Athens, more Italian than the natives of Napoli. Well-to-do Englishmen became ranchers in Alberta, but you could never call them cowpokes. The McLeod Hunt Club got successful turnouts, while elsewhere in the province genteel English expats shot grouse and rode to hounds, chasing after...coyotes. It's not like they were going to find a fox anywhere in the vicinity! One commentator of the era wrote: "The rough and festive cowboy of Texas and Oregon has no counterpart here...the genuine Alberta cowboy is a gentleman."

The strength of English feeling across the West is perhaps best shown in the way the young Winston Churchill was treated. Churchill was fresh from his adventures in the Second Boer War and his amazing escape in South Africa, having cranked out two quick books on his exploits and making a speaking tour across North America. His visits to the States didn't get him much, and he was surprised to run into American sympathy for the Boers.

In Winnipeg, however, he made more than $1500. It was in Winnipeg that Churchill also saw reaction to the death of Queen Victoria. "This city," he wrote his wife, "far away among the snows—fourteen hundred miles from any British town of importance began to hang its head and hoist half-masted flags." ✓

Unfortunately, the Americans had become a problem again. This time, their invasion was unofficial, but equally as destructive. If Alberta cowboys were gentlemen, American traders were not. They brought guns and trouble, often lubricated by whisky from distilleries in Chicago and St. Louis. They didn't call Fort Hamilton "Fort Whoop-Up" for nothing (the fort was located near what is now Lethbridge, Alberta). In May 1873, American hunters in the Cypress Hills massacred 20 Assiniboines. Law and order was desperately needed.

An English army officer was sent as early as October 1870 to check how bad things were. Lieutenant William Butler covered a gruelling 4400 kilometres by wagon, horseback and dog team and came back with a report he published under the title, *The Great Lone Land*, a name that became popular for the region for years. Butler had harsh criticisms over the booze trade affecting the Natives, and he recommended a mounted military force of about 150 men lay down the law in the wide-open spaces beyond Upper Canada.

The federal government sat on its hands and chose to send out another investigator, this time a colonel of the Canadian militia. He came back in December 1872 and told John A. Macdonald personally that Butler was right. The frontier was indeed wild and conditions deplorable.

In one year alone, 88 Blackfoot tribe members were murdered in drunken brawls. American traders were bringing in rifles, revolvers, whisky, anything they liked without a care for the laws that prohibited them or the customs duties.

Still Ottawa dragged its feet until the report got out into the public domain, and Macdonald knew he had to do something. So the North-West Mounted Police (NWMP) came into being in 1873. Their model was the Royal Irish Constabulary (RIC), a police organization that was the English answer to Irish republicanism. The RIC may have been loathed in Belfast, but the new force created along its lines was to become as much a symbol for Canada as the maple leaf. The reason why Mounties to this day wear red (these days just for the dress uniform) is because of a tie to England. Many Natives trusted their "old brothers"—the redcoat soldiers of Her Majesty's 6th Regiment of Foot stationed at Fort Garry. In a brilliant PR move, it was suggested the new police force capitalize on this trust.

What they were and the way they performed their job was truly amazing. They were expected to police vast stretches of terrain, often alone. Unlike American marshals and sheriffs, they were not elected but were representatives of the Crown. A Mountie was armed, unlike the famous Bobby on the streets of London, but there's something of the same English sensibility in the way they commanded respect from both settlers and Aboriginals.

As Pierre Berton wrote in his book, *The Wild Frontier*, "The Mounted Police were inviolable; it was useless to come up against them in the kind of *mano a mano* gunfight cherished by aficionados of the American West. For if one were shot, another would immediately take his place...until, in the finality, the long arm of justice (reached) all the way from Westminster...."

Like the early English policeman on the streets of London, the Mountie in the field often relied on his own judgement and ingenuity. A case in point is how officers dealt one time with Sitting Bull. We're all familiar with the heritage commercial in which the famous chief, brilliantly played by Graham Greene, tells off an American general in front of the two Mounties he respected, Commissioner McLeod and Major Walsh. His words were a little different, but this really *did* happen (and Walsh really did quit over Ottawa failing to help the starving Sioux in the cruel winter of 1880). But relations between the Native legend and the NWMP weren't always chummy.

A few of Sitting Bull's men once stole several of the force's mounts from a spot called Wood End. A single officer had been left to guard the horses, and the only thing he could do was fire a warning shot over the Natives' heads. Sitting Bull had the gall to actually send word round to the Mounties that he was upset with them firing on his warriors.

This didn't go down well with a sub-inspector named Allen, who took a collection of his men to the Sioux camp. Sitting Bull, sitting on a pony as he spoke with the officer, was completely defiant—no, he didn't intend to give the horses back. He didn't think the Mounties could take them back either.

"I would take the horse you are riding if I thought it stolen," Allen warned him.

"It is," Sitting Bull shot back.

His bluff called, Allen brought his horse next to the pony and lifted Sitting Bull right out of his saddle. Then he grabbed the animal's bridle and pulled it away. With the chief's men staring in amazement, Allen's Mounties closed ranks to protect him and then they galloped off for the safety of their fort.

A dramatic gesture is one thing. It's another to have a party of indignant Sioux warriors feeling disrespected and about to attack your base. The officers buried letters of farewell to their loved ones in an iron box. Lucky for them, Sioux chief Broad Tail was annoyed with Sitting Bull throwing his weight around, and he talked the warriors out of attacking the Mounties. No one is likely to make an *Historica Minute* out of that episode.

The most famous Mountie of them all had a sense of duty rooted in English family tradition. Sam Steele's family included a military ancestor who fought with Wolfe and another who was with Nelson at the Battle of Trafalgar; yet another was killed at Waterloo. Tall and barrel-chested, Steele was an officer who grew larger than life to fit the land. On more than one occasion, he faced down ugly mobs with little more than a Winchester rifle and the authority in his voice. He rose through the Mountie ranks to become a legendary figure at his various postings. In the Yukon, he was the law, keeping reasonable policies when it came to gambling and prostitution but willing to deport the incorrigible troublemakers in a flat second.

What beat him in the end was not any Western villain but the patronage system, which reeked from an eastern direction leading all the way back to the Rideau Canal. He went up against one of the cronies of Clifford Sifton, doing his best to block the man from getting on the Yukon's liquor licensing commission. Steele was head of the board and knew what kind of pork barrel came with the appointment. The outraged minister fired him from his post with a terse telegram. The Dawson City newspapers were united in heaping scorn on Sifton for the move and praising Steele of the Mounted.

Given his family's military background and his English roots, he was a natural choice to raise a unit of Mounties on leave to go fight the Second Boer War in South Africa. Later, a British royal commission proclaimed, "There was no better commander than the rough riding colonel from Canada."

His reputation, however, has been marred to some degree by recent scholarship. It suggests he covered up an incident when he and his men fired on Boers at a farm waving a flag of truce (six Boers were allegedly hanged on the spot). But with the end of the war, he apparently was suggesting his men learn Afrikaans and recommending weapons be returned to the Boers (of the majority black population, he seemed to be indifferent and held the racist attitudes of his times).

Steele's achievements or defects, ultimately, reflect on the man, but the legacy of the force—now the Royal Canadian Mounted Police—endures. The Mounties have been so beloved and revered in Canada (while occasionally facing harsh criticism) that they are a "brand" with RCMP-licensed merchandise. Ironically, their English roots proved to be the force's Achilles heel in what became arguably the greatest challenge the country faced in the latter half of the 20th century—but that's for a later chapter.

As the 20th century started, Canada was an infant nation, yet one that was bursting with all the marvels of the Victorian Age. Winnipeg had gone from an infamous spot of muddy streets without wooden planks—but plenty of brothels—to a boomtown with electrified streetcar service. Calgary was a little behind; signs warned guests of the Royal Hotel, "Do not attempt to light the bulbs with a match." Victoria boasted of having more telephone users per capita than any other North American community. In Toronto, financier Henry Pellatt was lighting the city streets and dreaming of building himself a castle (which he did with Casa Loma, but then Pellatt was an oddball—he once got false teeth manufactured for his horse).

All that prosperity, phone service and electric power meant options and widening perspectives. It meant people began to question what England meant for them since it clearly wasn't needed anymore for defence, not even as an essential trading partner—that honour went to the United States. Staying loyal to Mother England was a given, but there were rumblings for us to decide more of our own affairs.

One of those who complained was the Canadian master of humour, the man who wrote the famous line about an English lord "who flung himself upon his horse and rode madly off in all directions." Comedic writing was in his future. Just after the turn of the 20th century, Stephen Leacock was sober and serious about ties with Britain. He was, by his own definition, an imperialist, but he was one "because I will not be a colonial."

He was born in Swanmore, Hampshire. That really doesn't merit connecting him to English influence—far more interesting is *why* the Leacocks ended up in Canada. His father became an outcast after marrying without his parents' permission, which shut him out of a family fortune made in Madeira and an impressive mansion in Oak Hill on the Isle of Wight. And what could be more English than a rich son thrown out over a family scandal?

Leacock's father had charm but little else—not much talent or ambition—and he ended up running a farm near Sutton, Ontario. Young Stephen had a keen mind that took him far in Upper Canada College and then later as an academic. In fact, the textbook he wrote on political science brought him more money during his entire lifetime than any of his humorous stories and books. He might have only climbed in notoriety as the author of a few well-regarded textbooks—or perhaps he would have made a breakthrough in theory in his beloved economics—if he hadn't turned to humour.

But before *Nonsense Novels* and *Sunshine Sketches of a Little Town*, he was a talented lecturer. In 1907, Canada's governor general, Earl Grey, heard him speak in Ottawa and arranged for him to tour the Empire to promote unity. Leacock had his own ideas about imperial spirit. "We will be your colony no longer," he told a London conference. "Make us one with you in an Empire, Permanent and Indivisible." His presumption irritated the English, and Winston Churchill—once so impressed by loyal grief in Winnipeg over Queen Victoria's death—considered Leacock's opinions "offensive twaddle."

Churchill, of course, was always a lost cause. Those who approached Westminster and Parliament with reasonable requests for independence or self-rule were enemies in his book. Gandhi, to him, was a "half-naked fakir," and a politician from Burma looking for independence had to be a traitor. "Winston was often right," observed one of his inner circle, "but when he was wrong, well, my God."

Yet Churchill's how-dare-they attitude reflected a significant portion of how England's classes, both lofty and low, thought of these rebellious stirrings in the Empire. It was unfathomable to them, it smacked of ingratitude.

Canada may have been the most impenetrable of mysteries, when it was contemplated at all, because it was predominantly English in character.

It took a world set on fire in 1914 for the first great split in Canadian consciousness from the English idyll—a pointless slaughter that made Canadians reach for a new identity.

DON'T MENTION THE WAR

We were the nasty ones. We were the fighters the Germans learned to dread in the war that was supposed to end all wars. Today, we've cocooned ourselves in the comfortable myth, since the age of Lester B. Pearson, that we're a country of peacekeepers (when, in fact, as defence analyst Sunil Ram pointed out in a column for *The Globe and Mail* in 2004, for dozens of UN peacekeeping missions since 1948, we actually committed fewer than 100 military and civilian police and, many times, fewer than *10* personnel). Our military reputation used to be quite different, and that legacy started with the English.

Our role in the Great War was so crucial that British Prime Minister David Lloyd George recounted in his memoirs: "The Canadians played a part of such distinction (for the Battle of the Somme in 1916) that thenceforward they were marked out as storm troops; for the remainder of the war they were brought along to head the assault in one great battle after another. Whenever the Germans found the Canadian Corps coming into the line they prepared for the worst."

He was right. A German officer taken prisoner admitted, "The British, they are good soldiers but the Canadians, they are madmen."

Canada emerged from the trenches with a new confidence, and we arrived at the peace talks of 1919 as a signatory in our own right. So how did we get there? And how did boys from the wheat fields and logging camps and fisheries come to be the ones the Germans dreaded?

The world both before and during the Great War is almost unrecognizable. When we see photos and footage of crowds in public squares cheering the news that the war had started we can't help but shake our heads in pity at the coming nightmares these naïve souls could scarcely imagine: muddy, bloody, rat-infested trenches and shelling that could drive men nearly deaf and mad, a lunar landscape of ravaged earth and razor-sharp wire, with friends dying and suffering hideous amputations to gain a pitiful few metres of ground. And should you break, should your nerves crumble and you run for your life (though there's hardly any place to go), you would be shot by a firing squad. There was no such thing as empathy for those pushed past their psychological limits; in the early years of the war, you were branded a coward and that was that.

You also couldn't even criticize the idiot above you who, chances were, got his rank and command thanks to cronyism or nepotism. A trusted superior could often prove to be astonishingly incompetent. Just before the Battle of the Somme, one general warned his men:

"All criticism by subordinates…of orders received from superior authority will, in the end, recoil on the heads of the critics." The prevailing mentality was to kill the messenger.

Lloyd George mentioned the Somme, and indeed, the battle underscored the drastic need for change with how the whole Entente was fighting the war. For days, the British hammered the German lines with an incredible bombardment. The logic of the strategy went that an offensive along the River Somme would help the French, who were having a bad time at Verdun. A steady down-pour of shelling was supposed to cut the German wires, wreck the machine gun outposts and literally pulverize the Germans into submission so that British forces could stroll on in, meeting little resistance.

The truth was that, yes, the Germans were badly hurt by the pounding, but by this time they had developed an intricate, sophisticated warren of very deep trenches, many with creature comforts to make a long stay endur-able (after the war, the Allies were appalled upon discover-ing the difference between these often clean, comfortable hideaways and their own pitiful trenches). The Germans dug in and held on. British commanders who refused to hear such bad news as wire failing to be cut or gun out-posts still operable were the same oblivious fools about to send their men to a bloodbath on July 1.

On that day, in the early morning after a final barrage in which 3500 shells *a minute* had dropped on the enemy, the whistles blew, and thousands of soldiers went over the top. Loaded with 60-pound (27-kilogram) kit bags, sweating and anxious, they headed in the direc-tion of the breeze across the field. They had been told to *walk*. And if you think that's insane, you are absolutely right. The German guns could fire up to 500 bullets a minute—they might as well have been scything wheat. On the first day alone, 19,000 British troops fell with another 38,000 wounded.

No actual Canadian infantry units fought on that horrible first day, and any Canadian casualties were among the British divisions, but the 1st Newfoundland Regiment was literally wiped out. As the struggle for the Somme went on, the British commanders noticed the Canadian fierceness. For instance, the 22nd Battalion—the Van Doos—drove back 14 counterattacks, seven in one night alone. But the casualties across the British forces were so enormous that something finally *had* to be learned and things had to change.

The man who decided our military fate, the commander in charge of the Canadian Corps, was a seventh son of an earl from Hertfordshire with the nickname "Bungo." The background sounds like a recipe for yet another caricature of British incompetence out of the history sitcom, *Blackadder*. But Sir Julian Byng was nobody's fool. Despite his father's title, the family had little money, and it was only through ol' Dad knowing the Prince of Wales that young Julian found his way into a Hussars unit (meanwhile, the Prince of Wales and the rest of the royal family decided it might be better image-wise to change their German surname to *Windsor*).

Byng made do financially by training and selling polo ponies. Maybe the realities of work and the need to make a living gave him his down-to-earth frankness, because by the time he was commanding Canadians, he knew just the right way to talk to these men. Like them, Byng had an easy nonchalance and didn't even take his hand out of his pocket to return salutes. He ignored spit-and-polish to focus on whether a rifle actually worked and troops had what they needed. In India, he had ordered a change in soldier's jackets so that the high collars were done away with, and they could open them up in the stultifying heat. The Canadians loved him, even calling themselves "the Byng Boys."

Byng cleaned house in the Corps, ditching 15 out of 48 battalion commanders and two brigadiers who didn't measure up. He sent out men to go learn what they could from the British and French army units battered in the Somme and at Verdun. And his best move was mentoring Arthur Currie, the tactical genius who would become Canada's first full-rank general. Currie is rightly credited as the big brains behind landmark Canadian victories, but he worked closely with Byng, who believed—just as much as Currie did—in rigorous training, meticulous preparation and battle simulation exercises. The Canadian War Museum's Great War historian, Tim Cook, calls Byng the "single most important person in shaping the Canadian Corps during the war...."

Under Currie and Byng, Canadian soldiers became masters of the night raid, swooping into German trenches to collect prisoners. Their units competed to see who could pull off the most daring operations. As Cook writes in the second volume of his brilliantly comprehensive history of the war, *Shock Troops*, "In (some) cases, lone Canadian privates began to march back a dozen or more disarmed prisoners." With the Battle of Vimy, the Canadian reputation for tactical boldness was secured.

Back home, however, Canada was never fully united behind the war. It has to be remembered that a substantial number of men in the Canadian Expeditionary Force were originally from Britain. When Prime Minister Robert Borden wanted to shore up the numbers, his conscription bill was met with angry protests in Montréal. Not only was there Francophone defiance in Québec, there were protests as well in Winnipeg and Vancouver. Many of these men were the sole support for their families and the only ones available to work farms, and when all exemptions were cancelled, the Borden government faced bitter resentment. In the end, of course, these men had no choice but to don their uniforms.

Expediency was the order of the day. Because men were needed to fight for England, Borden—a typical sexist of the times—came out in favour of women having the vote in 1917, assuming they would back his conscription bill. The women, however, had to be related to soldiers to cast their ballots.

Having ensured Canada sailed over to fight for England, Borden was determined it also got a seat at the table for the peace. The French and the Americans cynically thought Dominion representatives were Britain's way of padding its votes at the Paris conference. This actually wasn't the intention at all. Lloyd George, a Welshman, understood very well that India, Australia and in particular, Canada, had played crucial parts in winning the war. Canada, Robert Borden wrote his wife, "was a nation that is not a nation. It is about time to alter it."

Today, the historians squabble over whether Canada's stronger national identity meant disillusionment with England and a decline in Imperialist sentiment. Frankly, it's hard to see how it couldn't have been so. Englishmen at home were disillusioned. Poet Siegfried Sassoon tore off his Military Cross ribbon and chucked it in the Mersey. Philosopher Bertrand Russell went to Brixton Prison for spreading pacifism. If the jumble of European conflicts that led to the war were enough to confuse a Kingston-upon-Thames lad, one who grew up with Calais right across the Channel, then they must have seemed even more remote to a depressed and mud-soaked infantryman fresh from Alberta.

As early as 1916, Manitoba MLA Fred Dixon, a Social Democrat, was telling an anti-registration rally at Winnipeg's Strand Theatre, "I am not afraid to die, but I want to know what I am going to die for. I am not going to die for a myth."

Many of the Canadians and English immigrants who walked out of those trenches, haunted yet victorious, didn't question England itself; for the country, they were still proud. They questioned the men who ran England, the institutions of privilege and wealth that had forced them to go. From now on, you couldn't demand a young man pick up a rifle just by waving a flag in his face; you needed a reason, a crusade. You also needed something to show for it, and Canadians wanted more say in how their affairs were run.

Field Marshall Douglas Haig met a delegation of them and called them a "well meaning but second-rate sort of people." But then Haig treated men as cannon fodder and was known as "The Butcher of the Somme."

Less than a year after the war ended, Frederick Dixon was in Winnipeg raising his voice for a different crusade, as what was called "The Soldiers' Parliament" grew in a radical, sometimes violent Winnipeg...

The Great War gave birth to a wealth of literature, songs and poetry, and the most famous poem of all from the conflict was, of course, composed by a Canadian: "In Flanders Field" by John McRae, a doctor who eventually achieved the rank of lieutenant colonel in the

Canadian Army. Few of us are probably aware that even this has an English connection.

In the spring of 1915, having survived the nightmare of Ypres, McRae was sitting on the back of an ambulance parked near a dressing station, grieving for a former friend and student killed by a shell. He scribbled his rhymes in his notebook and found inspiration in the wild poppies growing out of the earth that had been ripped and potholed by artillery fire. Like many a writer, he wasn't happy with his draft work and threw it away, but another officer fortunately scooped it up and submitted it to *The Spectator*. No joy there, but three years later, *Punch* liked the poem and published it. To this day, we still hear the poem at Remembrance Day ceremonies, and its phenomenal popularity can be traced right back to that most English of magazines.

The same year McRae sat on an ambulance, thinking of poppies, an English immigrant from Birmingham named Harry Colebourn sat on a railway car on his way to an army training camp in Valcartier, Québec. He was a veterinarian, and at a stop in White River, Ontario, he came across a hunter selling a black bear cub after shooting its mother. Colebourn shelled out $20, which was no small amount of money at the time, and smuggled the bear across to England, where it became the unofficial mascot for his brigade and later was adopted by the London Zoo.

You can guess the rest. A boy named Christopher Robin Milne loved the bear named after Colebourn's home city of Winnipeg. Zoo handlers, who were far more accommodating in the 1920s, let young Christopher into Winnie's cage. (Can you imagine any handlers who would pull a stunt like that today?) A.A. Milne chronicled the bear's fictional adventures, and Christopher

Robin later wrote one of the first "tell all" celebrity auto-
biographies complaining about what a hard life he had
growing up as a children's literature icon. The books and
the bear endure. Anyone who is a genuine fan knows
that, for all the calculated cuteness of Disney, the genuine Winnie is in the illustrations of E.H. Shepard and
rooted in the intriguing pleasure that once upon a time,
the bear was *real*.

Now a black bear cub purchased by an English vet
didn't create very much of Canada, not even that much
of Winnipeg. But it's stories like this that give a city its
flavour, just as the Golden Boy on top of the Manitoba
Legislature is much more interesting when you know it
was cast in bronze in France but sat around in a ship's
hold because the vessel was needed for the war. Foreign-
ers, if they know anything at all about Winnipeg (besides
fearing the climate), tend to recite from guidebooks that
the bear of "very little brain" is named after it.

True, it's not a big thing.

But it's a nice thing.

And so we're back to Winnipeg, where modern memory
hangs on to another part of the city's heritage, though
most people barely know or remember the historical
details: the Winnipeg General Strike of 1919. So soon
after the Bolshevik Revolution, Winnipeg became—albeit
for a short while—the centre of the universe as far as the
news was concerned. And again, the English were directly
involved. Believe it or not, they were actually painted as
the villains in the whole affair.

The crowd gathering in front of Winnipeg's old City Hall on June 21, 1919, "Bloody Saturday."

It was an age of fervent political belief, even as men came home from war no longer completely believing in nationalism. In England in the 1990s, I met an old English Communist Party member whose politics likely cost him advancement within the civil service, and I asked, "But why Communism?" After all, the cracks were always there, the lack of tolerance with dissenting opinion to the party line, the contradictory babble of Marxist doctrine always impenetrable (Bertrand Russell was pointing this out to the champagne crowd as early as the 1920s but no one wanted to listen).

With an avuncular patience, he explained, "You have to understand there was nothing else, no other alternative. If you believed in certain things, your only choice was to be a Communist."

Whatever the truth of that, veterans who fought and bled for their country felt a new sense of entitlement in 1919, and many were, indeed, disillusioned with King and Empire and the demoralizing prospect that things would go on just as they always had. If they were radicalized at all, it was out of desperation. There were few jobs, low wages, lousy housing, all while the rich stayed exactly that, never having risked their hides on the Western Front.

The strike was always an English creation. Strikers were inspired by the political successes of the Labour Party in England and the trade union movement there. More than half the leaders of the strike were English born. Fred Dixon, for instance, had come from the village of Englefield, near Reading, and George Armstrong, the only naturalized Canadian strike leader, was a descendant of United Empire Loyalists. The rest of the strike leadership was very much a Britons' club, with about a quarter of the leaders Scots and a sprinkling of Welsh and a few Irish. As for the rank and file in the protests, these were descendants of all those eastern European immigrants that Clifford Sifton lured into colonizing the West: Russians, Ukrainians and Germans, Eastern Orthodox Christians and Jews.

Boiled down to the basic issues, the strike was about metal workers in the city being granted union recognition and the demands of higher wages and a shorter work day. In May, the Trades and Labour Council put out the call for a general strike and brought the city to a virtual standstill. So many strikers, strike sympathizers and out-of-work men and veterans hung about Victoria Park for the speeches and rallies that they took to calling it "The Soldiers' Parliament." The firefighters and police were sympathetic and would have stayed on the picket lines as well, but the strike committees correctly understood they were needed to keep public order.

Not surprisingly, the newspapers—which saw an exodus of their printers and pressmen out the door to join the throng—indulged themselves early in Jew-baiting and slurs on immigrants, including the vulgarity of "Bohunk" for eastern Europeans. Socialism, which had taken over Russia, just had to be a Jewish or an Eastern European plot. Even the *New York Times* got itself into a tizzy, declaring, "Bolshevism Invades Canada." Then when that didn't wash, it became an English plot, and there were signs put up in shops that read, "English Need Not Apply." My grandfather still saw a few when he went looking for work in the mid-1920s as a new arrival.

Arthur Meighen, then the Solicitor General, also viewed the strike leaders as a band of revolutionaries who ran the gamut from "crazy idealists to ordinary thieves." Meighen had a keen mind that grasped complex mathematics and he was known for his sharp wit, but in terms of listening to the frustrations of the average working man, he was utterly tone deaf.

A federal law—as absurd as it was ruthless—was hastily passed to make it easy to deport the strike leaders. A Canadian at this time was a British citizen as well, with his passport using the same nationality code as a British one. So the government was overnight declaring an Englishman an alien in his own country and was ready to exile him back to his birthplace! It could only get worse. The authorities organized a special goon squad militia, arming its members with baseball bats. On June 17, the federal government dumped 12 union leaders into Manitoba's grim Stony Mountain Penitentiary and banned the publication of the strike newspaper, the *Western Labor News.*

The most infamous part of the crackdown was how Ottawa sent in the Mounties. On June 21, about 6000 protesters showed up for a strike rally and a parade organized by veterans. Instead of "Upholding the Right," the lawmen galloped their mounts down Winnipeg's Main Street, firing revolvers into the crowd and swinging bats. At one point, a mob tipped over a tramcar and set it ablaze—this became one of the iconic images of the strike. The other is of the Mounties riding and shooting indiscriminately. Two strikers were killed, many more were wounded in the violence and more than 30 arrests were made. What they soon called "Bloody Sunday" succeeded in breaking the back of the strike. On June 25, workers went back to their jobs, knowing that if they didn't, they would probably lose them altogether.

While Ottawa had brought in its immigration law, using the strike leaders' "Englishness" against them, they didn't count on one thing. Englishmen expect English justice. In late June, the Soldiers' and Sailors' Labour Party collected 365 names for a petition sent to Meighen, demanding the adherence to "those principles of Liberty and Democracy for which we volunteered to fight."

The government could get away with immigration tribunals for accused participants with European names, and one Oscar Chappelrei was promptly deported. It was not so easy to shut up the leaders like Dixon, Armstrong and Bill Pritchard who spoke in English, were eloquent and would get plenty of newspaper coverage. The government managed to charge and convict several of them of seditious conspiracy.

Years later, Pritchard recounted how a Scottish guard watched the radical prison inmates passionately argue politics while having a smoke. "Conspiracy?" he scoffed.

"Seditious conspiracy? My God, you fellows can't agree on any one point!"

Thanks to those Englishmen importing their trade union activism, Winnipeg was known for the better part of the 20th century as the West's haven for progressive ideas and left-wing ideology. For the rest of the century, there was a lot of self-indulgent romanticism written in newspaper columns and magazines about the North End of Winnipeg (which was rich, since the *Winnipeg Tribune* and the *Manitoba Free Press* were both against the strike). But there were truths, too, in the yarns spun about kitchen-table strategy sessions and marches past the Eaton's store on Portage Avenue. The activists in the 1920s were in genuine fear of arrests and worse. They really were risking everything.

The ghosts of a failed revolution still hang around north of Portage and Main, though the ethnic makeup of the neighbourhood has drastically changed. And you can still feel the tectonic shift in income and culture the minute you walk past the Museum of Man and Nature and the Manitoba Theatre Centre; the district has always had its share of pubs where blood on the floor mixed with the puddles of beer. For years, one of the silliest legacies of the Red scare era was that the RCMP kept a video camera in a popular leftist bookshop; whether it was there above the door to intimidate, or some officer honestly thought you were a danger to the country by picking up a paperback reprint of writings by the anarchist Bakunin, we may never know.

Roland Penner—today a distinguished Dean of Law for the University of Manitoba and the son of one of the strike organizers—had trouble crossing the border into the United States in the 1980s because he was a former

"Commie." At the time, he was a provincial cabinet minister!

Out of the fight for England in the war and new English radicalism, Winnipeg forged a self-image that included "leftist chic." It doesn't really matter what your politics are—it made the place more interesting. As a proud former Winnipegger myself, I can't help but think the war of ideologies suggested the city was the right place to start a theatre community, music festivals, an internationally renowned ballet company, film projects. Long after the strike had ended, the city had a new attitude and way of seeing itself.

ENGLISH ECLIPSE

Elizabeth II met him when she was a nine-year-old princess at Buckingham Palace, and he bid farewell to her father the king by putting a hand on the sovereign's shoulder (a definite protocol no-no). "I'll be seeing you, brother!"

A teenage Richard Attenborough sat in the London Palladium with his little brother David, both spellbound, listening to him lecture. Here was a real "Indian" telling them of the drastic need for conservation and of the beauty of the Canadian wilderness.

His contribution to the early environmentalist movement, decades before anyone coined phrases like "going green" or shamed you into composting, was considered immense. He was world famous, and movies and even animated films are still made about him. A full-size replica of the log cabin where he lived at Saskatchewan's Ajawaan Lake is on exhibit in Hastings

Museum in England. And there's a plaque up at Hastings Grammar School.

The Hastings references are the final clues, just in case you don't know the story—because the problem with this noble Native lecturing everyone on the majesty of the woods and the need for its protection was that Grey Owl wasn't a real Native at all. He was an incredible fraud. Grey Owl was born Archibald Belaney right in Hastings in that very English year of 1888 when Parliament first let bicycles on the streets (as long as they had bells) and Jack the Ripper went around terrorizing the London East End.

Even from childhood, Archie found it preferable to invent a past. His mother didn't want him, his drunk of a father certainly didn't want him, and his care was left to a couple of spinster aunts. Since George Belaney had tried his fortune in America (and failed), his son Archie went around telling people his father toured with Buffalo Bill's Wild West Show. His daydreams fuelled by adventure books on the Canadian wilderness, Archie at last got his wish to see the frontier after he tossed firecrackers down the chimney of his timberyard boss. Not the smartest of career moves. The aunts decided it was better to send the bright but misbehaving teenager on his way.

Fair enough. Our hero had a rough start, and he had the right spice of mischief in him to make him intriguing. After he landed in Halifax in 1906, it wasn't long before the English boy found his way to the Temagami region of northern Ontario to learn from the guides and trappers and start reinventing himself. But the second problem with Grey Owl is that in becoming a famous writer, his best work of fiction was always his life, and he simply wasn't a very nice person.

The fascinated teenager, Richard Attenborough, grew up to be a gifted actor and brilliant director, and he put Grey Owl on the big screen in 1999 in the person of Pierce Brosnan, who clearly was trying his best with a limited script—because *Gandhi* it ain't. The film glosses over the more ugly facets of the man's character. Belaney, like his father, was a drunk. The police once went looking for him because Grey Owl was throwing knives at passing trains. He was also a bigamist who abandoned his wives and children, and though the film ends with a stirring speech hinting at his real identity, the actual man never made any public admission of the truth. When he was found dying of pneumonia in his cabin, it was filled with liquor bottles and bottles of vanilla extract, the poor alcoholic's substitute for when he couldn't get the real thing.

Worse, there are reports he didn't mind at all inventing "war dances" and music, passing them off as authentic Native creations—something that justifiably ticked off the Ojibwa and Cree. They could overlook Belaney claiming to be a Native, as tribes had always adopted whites into their culture. It was something else entirely, something offensive, to claim to be a reputable source for culture.

So First Nations people saw through him; whites did not. To his credit, he later pushed for Natives to be hired as game wardens, believing they would be sympathetic to his conservationist cause. If anything of substance has survived, it was when he was unguarded and sincere in writing to his mother—after a separation of decades—about his life in the wild. Kitty Belaney had an objective sense of her son's talent, and she sent his letters off to the British magazine, *Country Life*. This was the beginning of his fame, and it wasn't long after his successful articles that the Canadian Parks Department adopted Grey Owl as the face of its programs. There were books. There were short promotional films for the department. When Grey Owl wrote about the wilderness, he weaved a spell over his devoted readers. Here's a line from his *Pilgrims of the Wild:*

"And the aged trees whose great drooping crowns loomed high above our heads, standing omniscient in the wisdom of the ages, seemed to brood and to whisper, and look down upon our useless vigil, in a mighty and compassionate comprehension."

It's prose that's purple, over the top, but this kind of stuff went over big in 1935.

He went on a book tour in England that same year. His great love, Anahareo, the woman who is immortalized for much of Richard Attenborough's film, was irritated by the idea of perpetuating his façade across the ocean. Grey Owl replied, "They expect me to be an Indian. I'd stand on my head if I knew that people would listen." He was determined to give them a show. Perhaps the strongest of all those who were taken in by his charm, she left him in the end.

When he came back from England, he was riding his highest wave of popularity—and yet he was never more vulnerable. A reporter from the *North Bay Nugget* tracked down one of his wives, who didn't mind saying exactly who and what Grey Owl actually was. He could have been disgraced, ruined. If it happened today, he surely would be, but then in our blogosphere age and relentless digging for smears, he would never have got so far to begin with. Incredibly, the paper's staff "spiked" the story. They shelved it away. The rationale went that what the man said about environmentalism was more important than boosting circulation and getting the scoop.

So he survived the brush with nearly being exposed, and he went on another tour of England and pressed his luck, walking right into Hastings. No one was the wiser, except the aunts, and one female friend from years gone by who agreed to keep her mouth shut. The tour exhausted him and his latest wife. While she was hospitalized, Belaney went back to his cabin where he grew steadily worse with pneumonia. Park rangers dragged him on a sled to a Prince Albert hospital, but it was too late. He died after three days. The *Nugget* was free to print the truth at last.

Grey Owl wasn't the first writer, of course, to find success by inventing a persona. It worked for the French novelist, Colette. Alice Sheldon—better known as James Tiptree Jr.—wrote letters to fans and fellow science fiction writers for years as her male alter ego. And Belaney certainly wasn't the first writer to be a miserable lout. Patricia Highsmith was a cruel misanthrope while Evelyn Waugh was a racist bully. Today, we have memoirists who make up whole lurid tales of drug abuse to be guests on *Oprah*. Sadly, it's difficult to find any of Grey Owl's books in print anymore, while books *about* him are easy to come by.

If the man was never real, his message of conservation was. Even the most hardcore urban of us today put up a hand against rampant logging of BC forests and are uncomfortable with what oil companies might do to valuable wildlife habitats. He changed the way we see things, changed our attitudes—and that's what every writer of any ambition wants.

For a while, the revelation of his fraud hurt the cause (not to mention his book sales), but the message had already taken root. It's impossible to imagine someone born in Saskatchewan or Ontario dreaming up so shameless an impersonation. And knowing what we do of the hardships endured by First Nations peoples in these years before they secured their rights, what local resident would want to carry off such a performance?

Ironically, it took an English imposter to forget himself to help create a lasting feature of our national consciousness, our instinctive protection of our country's natural beauty.

The 1920s and '30s seemed to be an age for English reinvention of identity. We think of the Group of Seven as so thoroughly Canadian that it almost comes as a surprise to learn three of its members were English imports. J.E.H. MacDonald was born in Durham and came to Canada when he was 14. Arthur Lismer was born in Sheffield and got his early artistic education in England and Belgium. Frederick Varley, from the same hometown, also looked for inspiration in Holland, and it was Lismer who convinced Varley to come to Canada.

Those aren't the names that regularly spring to mind. Our most famous artist, Tom Thomson—everyone knows those vivid reds and oranges that leap off his canvasses—was never a formal member of the Group. But if he hadn't died from a blow to his head in a mysterious canoeing accident, he would certainly have a place. Emily Carr wasn't a member either, but she's also associated with the Group, and her totem poles are unmistakable. People, of course, know A.Y. Jackson, and if Canadians don't remember who Lawren Harris is, you can almost guarantee at some point they have seen one of his landscapes, because *no one* has ever painted snow like he has. And the old joke goes on—one started by Lismer himself, quoting a child visiting an exhibit—that the most famous member of the Group of Seven was "Jack Pine."

Like the works of the Impressionists, the paintings of the Group are best viewed in person. Photographs never, ever give you the mind-blowing *texture*, the power that hits you from even the humblest of the small canvasses. Members of the Group liked to perpetuate the myth that their works were "fully Canadian" and that they betrayed no influences from the old schools of art or from Europe. From a publicity standpoint, that sounds great, but it wasn't true.

Those Sheffield lads, Lismer and Varley, took away the lessons of pure draftsmanship, if nothing else, from their training in England. As the 19th century drew to a close, Emily Carr made a pilgrimage to London, where "the bricks oozed heat, and the air—well, there wasn't any." She thought she could learn something from the Westminster School of Art, but after having spent time in San Francisco, where she thought of herself as English, she was disillusioned by being spoken to as a colonial. Later, her health suffered to a crisis point, with crippling headaches and nausea, and at an East Anglia sanatorium, she underwent electroshock treatment for "hysteria." When she got out, she sailed for home, feeling like a failure.

But she wasn't, and some good came of her time in England. Carr propped up her easel in the woods near St. Ives, Cornwall, and made her first experiments with woodland landscapes, painting the trees that she found "haunting." The artist who best captured the beauty of the BC forest wasn't fully formed yet, but she was already learning what didn't work and what might work.

Just as with Grey Owl, Emily Carr and the Group of Seven's accomplishments were mainly a reaction—in a less extreme and, of course, a politely Canadian way—*against* England, against what Harris called "Dutch windmills, canals...Barbizon leftovers and tidy, circumspect English pictures."

And like Grey Owl, the official members of the Group of Seven turned right around and captured the admiration of the Old Country.

"In all probability," wrote Merrill Denison, "the members...will be forced to exhibit in the United States and forget the Canadian audience which should be here for them but which is not. Perhaps, okayed by New York, their work may wander home long after they are dead and be prized, not because it is good, or because it is Canadian, but because some other country was told it was Canadian and said it was good."

You would be right to ask at the moment: who is this joyless, spiteful pill Merrill Denison? I am pleased to inform you he was a second-rate playwright who became a hack writer of corporate histories, grinding out books no one ever wanted to read on Ontario Hydro and the Bank of Montreal. No, you shouldn't have ever heard of him, and yes, you can go back now to not giving a damn what he thought. He's quoted here because a) this is what we do to ourselves as a people time and again, and b) he's so gloriously, stupendously *wrong*.

As art historian and Sotheby's man in Canada, David Silcox, points out, yes, the Group had its detractors like Denison, but the Canadian public was overall positive toward their work. We *liked* this stuff—we liked it a lot, and we didn't need to wait until the members were all dead. And as with the Impressionists, the Group's beautiful landscapes strike a particular chord with children.

It's true, however, that in a young country sparsely populated, a boost of international recognition is sure to be a godsend. It wasn't a case of a Canadian audience not being there, but of hearing the word. The Group members weren't about to forget about Canada either with any glow of admiration from New York. If anything, they didn't fare so well with their initial shows for the Americans. The English knew better. For an exhibition in Wembley in 1924, they weren't just told the works were Canadian and "said it was good"; they could see for themselves the obviousness of the quality.

One writer gushed, "Emphatic design and bold brushwork are the characteristics of the Canadian section; and it is here in particular that the art of the Empire is taking a new turn."

When the show was over, the Tate Gallery bought up Jackson's *Entrance to Halifax Harbour* and was considering the purchase of works by the others. It was the critical validation at Wembley that spread the word so well back in Canada. Wembley led to Carnegie—an important exhibition for the Carnegie Institute the following year in Pittsburgh.

The English didn't create Canada here, but they did pull back a curtain so we could look out our window. If we couldn't see the view at first light, that doesn't say anything about the English—it says something about us. And consider the irony of *that* for a moment. The English, so unrepentantly dismissive, at times, down through the ages (and we have enough examples right in this book), saw the astonishing beauty of those paintings.

Look at those paintings again sometime. It's the same with other great works of art or a book that touches your heart, a piece of music that speaks to you—you don't need a critic to tell you it's good. But sometimes you might need an English person or a friend from a foreign culture to show you where it is.

The inter-war period was an age of English eclipse in Canada, and contrary to what you might think, World War II took us further away from England, not closer to it. Yes, there were echoes from 1914 of the Commonwealth call to arms, and there were certainly scores of Canadian soldiers training in England, eager and willing to go save Britain, Europe and parts of Asia from Axis evil. What the war meant for the English creation of Canada, however, amounted to very little.

In World War II, our soldiers wouldn't be heroes of famous battles like Vimy, grateful for English praise. We became liberators of nations, helping to free Italy and the Netherlands. Is there any sight so humbling and yet can fill you with such pride as when Canadian television broadcasts Remembrance Day ceremonies in Holland? The Dutch are grateful to Canadians. They do not forget over there. Nor should we.

But as early as 1940, Prime Minister Mackenzie King arranged a shotgun wedding for us with a new partner for our national defence. He met with America's Franklin D. Roosevelt on the president's private railway car near Ogdensburg, New York, and signed Canada up for a joint military agreement with the United States. So much for ties to England; we had a new supporting role in the Cold War drama that played out over the next 50 years.

In discussing English influence, we can't forget the remarkable, baffling opposites, the men who were born in this country and who were driven to make themselves English, even while the English identity seemed to wane in Canada. Their names are famous and infamous: Beaverbrook, Thomson, Black. It's uncanny how each one chose the same path, not just to make their fortunes in journalism and publishing but to use this to insinuate themselves into British society.

The first, and the one who climbed the highest, was Max Aitken, the first Lord Beaverbrook. In later life, he portrayed himself as the small-town poor boy made good, but he actually grew up in a large house as the son of a Presbyterian minister in Newcastle, New Brunswick. From his teens, Aitken had an impatient, entrepreneurial streak, dabbling in all sorts of ventures and sometimes fixing his wagon to the political star of his old teacher and mentor, R.B. Bennett. England wasn't so much a dream as an escape for Aitken. There's a stack of evidence to suggest he ripped off his investors in trying to create a cement firm monopoly in Eastern Canada, and in 1910 as the federal government asked tough questions, he quietly moved his family—along with his fortune—across the Atlantic, where he bought a controlling interest in Rolls Royce.

You can buy your way into society any number of ways, but it sounds appropriate to get a stake in the cars the rich drive, doesn't it? Soon Aitken was hobnobbing with his fellow New Brunswicker and future British prime minister, Andrew Bonar Law. As a British citizen, Aitken could run as a Conservative candidate in a riding near Manchester. He later told the CBC that Bonar Law secured him a knighthood for "the purposes of rewarding me for services to come."

Aitken plunked down £25,000 on a mansion called Cherkley Court near the small town of Leatherhead in Surrey and then invited the powerful and the culturally influential to come visit: Lloyd George, Yeats, Kipling, H.G. Wells and naturally, Winston Churchill. Meanwhile, he started buying up newspapers like London's *Evening Standard* and *Daily Express*. As the Great War was ending, he was made a Lord, taking his peerage name from a stream that ran near his hometown in New Brunswick.

Beaverbrook was a peculiar figure. He seemed to crave power and influence, but preferred being the puppeteer rather than the front man. His newspapers were always weapons of propaganda; they were "unloaded guns. But teach the man behind them how to load and what to shoot at, and they become deadly." They did, indeed, and he used them to smear his enemies. As a press baron, he loved having the ear of cabinet ministers, but he was distant to his wife and children, and when he was done fooling around with a Dutch–Javanese model, his son took her on as his mistress. As a Minister of Information during the Great War, he was well suited to shaping the Empire's propaganda machine, but he doubtless loved the access he had to key intelligence files.

There were those who despised him as an odious little colonial, yet he adopted all the political prejudices of an imperialist Englishman—pushing for free trade within the Empire, firmly against an independent India and preferring Britain stay on the sidelines while Europe figured out what to do about Hitler. During the Wallis Simpson crisis (when the infamous lady barely hid her affair with Hitler's foreign minister, Joachim von Ribbentrop), he tried to persuade Edward VIII—an idiot with his own Nazi sympathies—to stay on the throne.

And yet Beaverbrook never forgot about Canada. He was perhaps the best promoter of the Canadian contribution to the Great War. He created the Canadian War Memorial Fund, which hired British and Canadian artists to paint battle scenes, and he organized the Canadian War Records Office in London. It was England who made him a press baron with such a wide reach, and he used it to lift up the stature of his country of birth. As Churchill's Minister of Aircraft Production and later his Minister of Supply during World War II, he had a lot to do with saving England itself from invasion and turning the tide of the conflict.

But when it was over, Britons promptly voted—and voted big—to get Churchill out of office, recognizing he wasn't the man to lead them out of the bomb rubble into the new age. Beaverbrook, rudderless without a circle of great men in power, decided to come home to New Brunswick and start building memorials to his own posterity. Yes, rather than establishing his reputation and fortune in England, he might have stayed in Canada and acquired his wealth here (if he could have managed to stay out of jail). That might have allowed him to be the Chancellor of the University of New Brunswick. And he might have still built his art gallery and the Fredericton Playhouse without his English life. But he probably wouldn't have earned such awe from his fellow New Brunswickers without his career in Whitehall and his kingdom on Fleet Street, achievements that granted him a whole new influence back in the province.

A Fredericton travel writer, Colleen Thompson, says she was "like every other kid in Fredericton, brought up with the idea that Lord Beaverbrook was close to God." But H.G. Wells, who knew the man, never confused him with a deity. He famously commented, "If ever Max gets to Heaven, he won't last long. He will be chucked out for trying to pull off a merger between Heaven and Hell after having secured a controlling interest in key subsidiary companies in both places, of course."

Roy Thomson, unlike Beaverbrook, really did come from humble beginnings. He was the Toronto son of a hotel barber, a school dropout, and if he was destined to run a media empire, it was because he was so terrible at everything else. Bad eyesight kept him out of the army in the Great War, and a scheme to be a Prairie farmer ended in failure. He was lousy, too, at trying to distribute auto parts. He wound up in northern Ontario selling radios, but when he learned his market region had no stations to listen to, he bought a frequency and a transmitter for $200 and started CFCH in North Bay.

Now there is sure to be a reader out there who will remember Thomson had Scottish roots, and he bought up *The Scotsman* and launched Scottish Television. True, but the heart of the Thomson media empire would in time be on Fleet Street, right in the heart of England, and its jewel would be *The Times*. His domain became international in any case. He wound up owning *The Globe and Mail* along with a whole collection of other Canadian newspapers, British broadsheets and *The Jerusalem Post*, as well as the Hudson's Bay Company, a travel business that's become an empire today in its own right, book publishing firms and a North Sea oil and gas exploration business started with J. Paul Getty.

He was in so many ways an "anti-Beaverbrook" (and Max Aitken condescendingly dismissed his accomplishments). Unlike Aitken, he made his millions late in life.

Unlike Aitken, he cared nothing about the direction his newspapers took, declaring, "Editorial content is the stuff you separate ads with." While Beaverbrook gave his money away, Thomson wanted to hang onto it and make more. He had no interest in charity (the foundation that bears his name was created by others), and he revelled in his reputation as a penny-pincher, telling reporters to use scrap paper rather than notebooks. In Canada, he earned strong resentment for keeping wages low and for his clock-watching, but he was mostly considered fair and reasonable. If his best talent wanted to move on, he openly encouraged them.

He asked people to call him Roy and was known for being unfailingly polite and accessible, a trait his son and heir Kenneth had as well. Pear-shaped, wearing Coke-bottle glasses and unable to drive, he thought nothing of going down into the London Tube each weekday to head to his office. When I was a child, my father told me about Roy Thomson as an inspirational tale; Thomson had my same genetic defect causing extremely poor eyesight, and it was implied that if I were to overcome this, I could go on to great things like he did (no one, however, has sold me a television network lately or offered me a seat in the House of Lords).

In writing about his financial empire, journalist Susan Goldberg hit the nail on the head in observing there were two Roy Thomsons. "While the Canadian Roy Thomson had been snubbed by the newspaper establishment for regarding his papers solely as cash boxes and not as instruments for shaping public policy, the U.K. Roy Thomson had bought prestige when he purchased the *Times* papers."

And that seems to be the heart of the matter for why Roy Thomson was in England at all. In Canada, he could be shut out, ignored, discouraged, no matter how many papers he bought up. Sir Denis Hamilton, his *Times* editor-in-chief and later a chairman of Reuters argued, "I resent the fact that Toronto is inclined to write off Roy Thomson as a 'little man'…I tell them they're jealous, and there is a stunned silence. Within a short time of Roy's coming to London, he became very greatly loved and respected and in terms of commercial success, he was a colossus. Every single newspaper Roy bought in the United Kingdom was bigger than any he had had in Canada. What chance is there for spectacular judgement in news coverage in a place like Moose Jaw?"

Not to pick on Moose Jaw, but he was right. And here is a knighted member of the Brit establishment firmly on point about our own levels of snobbery.

Roy Thomson's coming to England was a breath of fresh air on Fleet Street. While he apparently had no problems with expenses when editors needed to chase a story, he put his bloated British papers on a lean financial diet, something unheard of (and something badly needed as the first rumbles of change in the industry were being heard in the 1960s, eventually driving the papers out of central London altogether).

The previous owner of *The Times* was a Lord Kemsley, who lived on a massive estate where servants brought him wire dispatches on a silver tray and who had the hallway of the office cleared for his daily arrival at the newspaper. Roy Thomson was modest, a boss who sincerely believed the receptionist was the most important person in a company as its first impression, a widower who dined by himself and who only indulged his enormous wealth in buying detective novels.

He didn't seem to care much about becoming a member of the House of Lords. Asked what he did there,

Thomson admitted, "Very little. I can't spare the time from my business to attend sessions, and I don't like to talk superficially. If I stand up to make a speech there, I want to have something to say."

By this time, 1964, the laws had changed, yet there was no fuss over Thomson's lordship like the one in Canada that followed with Conrad Black. But then people *liked* Roy Thomson, even knowing he was cheap and a businessman who drove hard bargains. His English employees liked him. The English elite liked him. You could talk to this media baron, one who made his own pursuit of money into a party joke, quipping, "The most beautiful music to me is a spot commercial at ten dollars a whack."

His son Kenneth told reporter George Tombs, "Under the laws of Canada at that time, it was not possible to have dual citizenship, and my father lost his Canadian citizenship when he became a British citizen.... My father continued to regard himself as a Canadian and hoped to finish his life in Canada, but regretfully, that did not happen."

Conrad Black never had the common touch like Roy Thomson—nor did he want it. His ancestors made their fortunes in booze and insurance in Winnipeg, but he was born into Canada's financial capital in the 1940s, Montréal. Black's father was a firm monarchist, and with the death of George VI, he took the family to England on what the shipping lines called a coronation cruise. They stayed at Claridge's Hotel, and the impressionable boy watched horse-drawn carriages make their way to

Westminster Abbey where Elizabeth II waited to be crowned.

When the Black family moved to Toronto, Conrad hated the desolate country that was then the city's Bridle Path, and he loathed Upper Canada College. The media tycoon who was convicted of fraud got an early start in business—and was first nicked by authorities—when he stole final exam questions and sold them to other students for $1400.

He dreamed big, and his heroes had big egos: Napoleon, Wellington, Roosevelt (his early sympathies were liberal). Toronto was too small for him. He studied the careers of both Beaverbrook and Thomson. "The trappings of aristocracy had appealed to Black for many years," George Tombs wrote in his book, *Robber Baron*, pointing out that Black "had grown up in a world of English–Canadian tycoons, like Bud McDougald and E.P. Taylor, who fawned on titled aristocracy. In 1982, four years after Black's takeover of Argus Corp., he applied to the Duke of Norfolk and the College of Arms for a newly designed coat of arms."

Black's rise and fall with Hollinger Inc. is so well known that we don't need to recount them here. It's his fascination with the trappings of the upper-class English world that concerns us. Once he bought the *Daily Telegraph*, he had his way in, the doors opening for him everywhere—even at Chequers, where on a visit, he gushed his admiration to then British Prime Minister Margaret Thatcher. As his influence grew, however, he began to irritate the English in the same way Beaverbrook had.

Black had evolved into a neo-conservative whose attacks in print on the liberal left and on reporters who offended him were strident and sometimes outright vicious. He took the view that Britain belonged in NAFTA more than it belonged in Europe, a position that even many conservatives in the U.K. find perverse and impractical. But he was established now where he always wanted to be, and he even had an English wife, Barbara Amiel, the poor Jewish girl from Watford who went from hard-left sympathies as an immigrant in Hamilton, Ontario, to hard right as an inflammatory, conservative columnist for *Maclean's*.

And then came his feud with Canada's Prime Minister Jean Chrétien, who spoiled all the joy of a peerage by bringing up an obscure and inconvenient legislative apostrophe known as the Nickle Resolution. Pick a Canadian off the street today, and he or she can't tell you what it is. Why should they? It's not even a law, just a policy from 1919 against Canadians adopting foreign titles. Black claimed Chrétien's obstinacy was personal, and he may have had a point as his newspapers offered no love for the Liberals. Citizen Black has long been infamous among reporters for what they call "libel chill," when a terse letter threatening court action is enough to make a journalist back off a story. So Black sued. He lost. He appealed. He lost again, with the Ontario Court of Appeal reminding him that the prime minister was entitled to give his recommendations to London and that "No Canadian citizen has a right to an honour."

He didn't just relinquish his citizenship. The battle ended with a nasty public rejection of his birthplace—a move that Beaverbrook wouldn't have risked and Roy Thomson would never have felt. Canada, Black fumed, was "an oppressive little world" with "a deteriorating currency." No longer a Canadian, he got what he wanted, to be a baron in name and not just in assets.

When the American courts started indicting the Lord of Crossharbour, he quickly wanted such insults forgotten. "He loves Canada," insisted his lawyer, Edward Greenspan. "Obviously, Canada is dear to him in many senses." Yes, we all saw how dear it was to the man who went from the House of Lords to the Big House, a low-security penitentiary in Florida.

As for the Baronness, once loathed by liberals for her extreme opinions, now Barbara Amiel could be hated for the lurid tales that came out over her extravagance, which she admitted to *Vogue* "knows no bounds." Both Mr. and Mrs. Black have kept using the papers to defend him. Instead of his heroes, Napoleon and Wellington, he conjures different names now. He wrote in the *National Post* that "if saintly men like Gandhi could choose to clean latrines, and Thomas More could voluntarily wear a hair shirt, this experience won't kill me."

Canadians, no doubt, will think of Conrad Black in the same breath as the Mahatma when they compare Don Cherry with the Dalai Lama.

So, three Canadian press barons, and what are we to make of them? England played a role in their creation—or rather their reinvention of themselves. Beaverbrook lusted for Whitehall influence. Thomson needed Fleet Street for the big deals he relished so much. And Black craved the pageant of England while admiring American drive; now he's a cautionary tale in vanity (down but not yet out). Their contributions to Canada are better assessed on one of those balance sheets that Roy Thomson loved so much. Their importance here is what they show us about ourselves, about how badly English respect was once needed for Canadian enterprise.

Kenneth Thomson must have understood how his country was changing. Oddly, Roy Thomson had insisted his son keep the title, but the second Baron of Fleet only used it in Britain, relying on two sets of stationery and Christmas cards. In Canada, he was plain Kenneth Thomson, polite and humble to strangers, and as a fixture of Toronto's upscale Rosedale neighbourhood, he often walked dogs for the Toronto Humane Society.

An upstart can be an irritant for the English elite, whereas the relentless Anglophile can annoy his fellow countrymen at home. For John Diefenbaker, his insistence on Queen, Commonwealth and Christianity was an all-or-nothing proposition. Strange, since the paternal roots of "The Dief" were German; on his mother's side, he had Scottish ancestry, but it was removed by a couple of generations.

His immediate family history had a bigger stake in the Canadian past, with relatives on both sides of the Upper Canada Rebellion of 1837. You can't even chalk up the Anglo worship to the war patriotism of his early years—he never even got to fight for the Empire in the Great War, an injury reducing him to the status of medically unfit and sending him home. But as a candidate in the federal election of 1926, he shouted to a crowd, "I want to make Canada all Canadian and all *British!*"

As Peter C. Newman once wrote, "No better definition of the true roots of his foreign policy was ever uttered by John Diefenbaker...."

He was a small-town lawyer who used stagey gestures in court, a simple man who grew up in Saskatchewan and who had simple tastes with a love for potatoes and TV wrestling. Yet he had his moments of wit. Someone compared the sprucewood house where he grew up to

Lincoln's log cabin. Without missing a beat, Diefenbaker said it was more like a manger. In some ways, he was stuck in the 19th century—the same way Winston Churchill often was.

But just as it's been said of Churchill, there was a slice in the layer cake that was of the 21st century. It was Diefenbaker who finally cleaned up the shame of First Nations peoples being denied the right to vote. It was Diefenbaker who, yes, scrapped our technologically brilliant Avro Arrow but who feuded with Kennedy over the Cuban Missile Crisis. He stood up to racist South Africa trying to weasel its way back into the Commonwealth. You would think the prime minister who backed the Canadian Bill of Rights could appreciate English heritage like a Leacock and want to see a uniquely Canadian emblem.

He didn't. It's hard to understand today what all the fuss was over the Great Flag Debate, but it was a bitter, name-calling, protracted battle in the House of Commons that Diefenbaker hated to lose. Facing him across the Commons floor was Lester Pearson, a war veteran, once a gifted athlete at rugby and hockey, and a skilful diplomat who had already won the Nobel Peace Prize. This cerebral former university professor was never comfortable as a politician kissing babies, and he vaguely sounded like Elmer Fudd. He was gambling that his listless Liberal government could find its way back on track with a symbol that unified Canada.

Right up until the 1960s, it was either the Union Jack or the Canadian Red Ensign that flew over government buildings and served as our national flag. We had none of our own. Pearson, recognizing Canada's new place on the international stage, also understood the practical necessity. During the Suez Crisis of 1956, Egyptian diplomats explained to him how their ordinary people couldn't distinguish Canadian troops from British ones.

The majority of Canadians wanted a new flag, and the country had evolved so that Pearson's Defence Minister, Paul Hellyer, could confidently suggest that "those of us of English stock, whether we like it or not, are in the minority in this country."

We might have got something very different than what we ended up with. Fortunately, the clunky design of three red maple leaves with blue borders—what Diefenbaker called "Pearson's Pennant"—lost out in a committee vote to a sleeker design of a single maple leaf with red borders.

On the morning after the new flag was first flown, journalist George Bain remarked that our new emblem "looked bold and clean, and distinctively our own." In a peculiar way, this sort of echoes the affection we built for the works of the Group of Seven: simple yet bold, vivid and unique. It was not the Union Jack with its heavy freight of associations, and it wasn't the loud, cluttered design of stars and stripes, so fitting for an America that was quickly acquiring its own baggage of accusations over imperialism. But Diefenbaker still didn't want it, and in fact, when he died in 1979, he was buried with his coffin draped with the new flag and then the Red Ensign he treasured.

So, by 1965 we had our own flag, our own military reputation, our own government institutions, a culture that grew partly out of English traditions but was (and still is) finding its plodding way toward a unique identity. After more than 40 years, Dief's reactionary crusade to hold onto the Red Ensign seems even more the bluster of a man out of step with a modern age, as if his was the last Anglophile hurrah. But the English—and not just English Canadians but the British English—were about to be the target and made the centre of a controversy that almost tore the country apart.

THE CRUELLEST MONTH

O n an autumn day in 1970, out near the Longueuil station of the Montréal Métro, police were waiting for a bushy-haired man of 27 who was expected to drop off a communiqué for his terrorism cell. Sure enough, he showed up, and the police followed him, but their suspect figured out he had a tail. Instead of rushing to the location where his accomplices were holed up, he went to the home of a couple who were friends and sympathetic to the cause, where he began donning a disguise. He used white shoe polish on his hair and hit himself again and again in the face with a brick wrapped in a towel so that it would swell up. When an "old man" stepped out of the house later, the police didn't recognize him and let him go on his way.

This was how one of the main perpetrators of the October Crisis slipped temporarily through the fingers of the Québec authorities.

And if you didn't know that about the October Crisis, there's probably a whole lot more you don't know.

We can start with a misconception that has somehow inserted itself into our collective national memory—the idea that tanks rolled into Montréal during the Crisis. They never did. There were no tanks at all. Common sense should refute this from the get-go if we remember a basic fact; anyone who has ridden a car in Montréal even well into the 1980s knows how cracked and pot-holed the streets of the city once were. Tanks would only have made that worse, and instead, personnel carriers and trucks were used to bring in troops.

The October Crisis is as much a narrative that says how the English created Canada as any others told in this book. It was a test of wills between terrorists and the federal and Québec governments. It was a struggle for the soul of a "distinct society" or a "nation within a united Canada" or however you choose to define the province. And the kidnapping of British diplomat James Cross and the murder of Québec minister Pierre Laporte was a suspense thriller with bizarre plot twists that would never be accepted by readers of fiction.

That includes the fact that one of the Cross kidnappers wasn't Québecois at all—he was a British-born engineering student, one who got away with his crime for a decade.

The Crisis is still very much with us. As recently as 2001, one of the original members of the *Front de libération du Québec* (FLQ), Rhéal Mathieu, who was convicted in 1967 of manslaughter for his role in a bombing of a shoe company, went back to jail again over attempted fire-bombings of Second Cup restaurants in Montréal. You can go on the Internet today and find blog comments that argue the Crisis and even the FLQ Manifesto must have all been a fabrication of the RCMP. They are reminiscent of those who believe men never walked on the Moon and point to a waving flag in the Apollo film footage (forgetting that in space, the laws of motion and of inertia still apply). That history can be shaped by an individual's choices, by turns of circumstance and plain dumb luck, doesn't seem to occur to these firm believers. What is truly sad is that if you walk into an Indigo's or Chapters bookstore today, you will find only one or two books in English print devoted to the October Crisis.

The FLQ wanted to kidnap an English citizen, a symbol. They wanted revolution against English companies, English government traditions and the English language itself. Today, even those in English Canada, especially the young, see the invoking of the War Measures Act as Canada's own version of martial law, a needless crackdown when it was nothing of the kind.

Much of what we've discussed throughout this book all came to a head in 1970, all the clouds of the past, all the old grievances and glories, all the unfinished business rolling and mingling together for a violent storm: the conquest of New France, the French laws allowed to continue under English colonial rule, the Lower Canada Rebellion, the Durham Report.... Even our "party king" from our first chapter, Charles II, has a legacy for the October Crisis. So as you read over events that took place in Québec decades ago, you may think you're only reading about an episode in the life of one province and about one people. Oh, no. This drama has plenty of French actors, but it is very much about the English. It's vital we understand that, because if we don't, we've failed to understand our country at all.

We need to start with the Québec that few English in the rest of Canada ever saw. It was a province that after World War II was mostly a backward state with rampant poverty, run—more like ruled—by Premier Maurice Duplessis in the same corrupt and autocratic style Huey P. Long ran Louisiana. Duplessis had no problem with the Roman Catholic Church keeping a tight grip on the province's education, and the church was infamous for its slogan, "*Le ciel est bleu; l'enfer est rouge.*" It means "Heaven is blue (the colour of the ruling Union Nationale); Hell is red (that is, Liberal)." Nor did he mind letting English–Canadian and foreign companies plunder their fill of Québec's resources. The language of business in Québec was English. When Canadians to the west and east carped about Québec demanding "more and more" from Ottawa, they either never knew or simply forgot the province was emerging from a Dark Ages.

After Duplessis died, Québec's Liberals finally got their chance and won the provincial election in 1960. What's now called "The Quiet Revolution" started with economic and social reforms and with services finally being secularized. The revolution didn't stay quiet for long. All the grievances, so long bottled up, shattered the fragile glass of the status quo, and unions for taxi drivers, police, factory workers, postal workers, you name it, were demanding change.

Demonstrations were often marred by violence. The October Crisis would not be the first time the army had been called in to Montréal. In 1969, when the city's police went on an illegal strike, taxi drivers held a violent protest at the headquarters of the much-loathed Murray Hill Limousine Company, which held a monopoly on service from Dorval Airport. There were dozens of injuries, and the firm's armed security guards fired into the crowd. A plainclothes police officer was killed, shot in the back. The soldiers were sent in.

The time for quiet was gone. People were demanding to know why top jobs at CN Rail were only going to Anglophones—and they asked quite loudly. They wanted to know why they couldn't get served in French when they walked into Eaton's department store. They resented Queen Elizabeth II visiting Montréal and reminding them of Canada's colonial heritage.

And many wondered why their province should stay in Canada at all. From the beginning, the issue of separatism was being pursued through peaceful political action. It found its strongest voice through René Lévesque, who helped found the Parti Québécois. Lévesque—constantly smoking, always slightly rumpled, articulate and fluently bilingual—was already famous to many in Québec as a popular broadcast reporter and interviewer. Had he wanted to, he could have let his impressive career of reporting on the London Blitz and on the Korean War take him to a top spot with America's broadcasters. Once a provincial Liberal, he no doubt could have carved out a place in federal politics. Instead, his efforts in the Quiet Revolution led him to fight for an independent Québec.

One of his fellow reformers was now his main rival: Pierre Trudeau. Both were educated by the Jesuits and both went to law school—only Trudeau finished and got his degree. While Lévesque was tagging along with combat units as a war correspondent in Europe, the young Trudeau was snubbing the discipline forced on him by conscription and riding around on a motorcycle, wearing a Prussian helmet. As a left-wing activist and intellectual in the '60s, it was natural the law professor from

Montréal would be wooed by the Liberals, and his rise was rapid within the party and the Pearson cabinet. The English who voted for him as prime minister in 1968 during the wave of "Trudeaumania" saw him as a federalist who understood Québec from the inside and could keep it in line. Militants in Québec now saw him as a traitor to their cause of separation. ✓

But separatism hadn't got very far in the elections. (It still wouldn't by 1970, when the Parti Québécois won just 23% of the vote and six seats in the National Assembly—Lévesque didn't even manage to win his own riding.) As early as 1962, there were those who decided a violent solution was needed, and out of the ragged, loose strands of several radical factions arose a band of dangerous amateurs.

They were, by turns, almost pathetically incompetent and chillingly, ruthlessly efficient. About 200 bombs were set off over the next seven years, including at the Montréal Stock Exchange and the mayor's residence, along with a rash of bank robberies. They expressed next to no remorse for their victims, starting with their first one, a night watchman named William O'Neill killed by a bomb planted behind an army recruitment centre on Sherbrooke Street West.

The news reports from that time and still today make much of the fact that O'Neill was a war veteran. More pertinent are the facts that O'Neill was fully bilingual and had a French Canadian mother. The FLQ's very first victim was an individual who was not quite but close to being one of the very people it claimed to champion. During a robbery of a firearms company, an FLQ member didn't hesitate to gun down a worker who had walked in, unaware of what was going on.

Scores of FLQ members were caught and tried during those years, and as mentioned earlier, their incompetence could sometimes border on the darkly comical and absurd. In 1964, *l'Armée Révolutionnaire du Québec* was founded by a 32-year-old Hungarian named François Schirm, who once belonged to the French Foreign Legion. Schirm started a training camp in the woods of the Mauricie region. He took a trip into Québec's forests and declared, "What ideal country for underground war! Here is the perfect bushland for partisans! Nobody could hunt out the revolutionaries here!"

Except for the provincial police and the Canadian army—who could always get helicopters, who could easily consult topographical maps of the parklands and forests and who could probably make educated guesses as to where the most likely sites of camps would be. And if all else failed, they could always wait for Québec's notorious winter. *Bon chance!*

In 1968, several of the key players in the national drama to come were all at a major evening event. It was June 24, St. Jean-Baptiste Day, and Pierre Trudeau ignored critics who urged him to stay away from the celebrations and the parade in Montréal. He saw no reason to hide. The city was his birthplace, his federal riding was here, and he was a proud Québecois. But emotions were running high, and hardcore separatists began throwing rocks and bottles at the review stand. Riot police clashed with demonstrators; 300 of them were arrested and 100 injured. Those watching the live television feed on CBC saw Montréal's mayor Jean Drapeau try to persuade Trudeau to flee the review stand. Trudeau refused—a brave move that's been interpreted as helping to fuel the Liberals' election win the next day.

The future kidnap victim, British trade commissioner James Cross, was also on the review stand that night. So was one of the FLQ's original targets, American consul Harrison Burgess. Below them, in the shouting, angry crowds fighting those riot police truncheons were schoolteacher Paul Rose and taxi driver Jacques Lanctôt, who were taken away in the same paddy wagon. This is how they met. They later appeared together on television, protesting the police's brutal crackdown that evening.

Meet the two masterminds of the FLQ behind the October Crisis.

Yet what followed came close to being prevented from ever happening at all. On February 6, 1970, Montréal police pulled over a rented van driven by Jacques Lanctôt, whom they already knew was part of the FLQ, with an accomplice along for the ride. They searched the back and found a sawed-off shotgun and a wicker basket large enough to carry a human being. On the seats were documents that suggested Lanctôt and his accomplice planned to kidnap the Israeli consul Moshe Golan. They were arrested on a weapons charge and for conspiracy. But the kicker is that Lanctôt was *actually granted bail.* Of course, he jumped it.

Then in June, police raided a house in Prévost, north of Montréal, and discovered $28,000 in cash from a recent bank job, more weapons, plus bombs and detonators. Even more chilling was the FLQ communiqué that outlined a plot to kidnap the American consul. Lanctôt's brother François was arrested, and this time, somebody had the good sense to make sure bail wasn't an option. Police even turned up a map that led to the FLQ cell's farmhouse in Sainte-Anne-De-La-Rochelle in the Eastern Townships, and the next day they came within minutes of catching three of the men who would be the main instigators of the Crisis—Rose, Lanctôt and Francis Simard. The trio raced in a panic to a hiding spot on the second floor.

According to James Cross, a general warning—incredibly—was never issued to diplomatic officials in Montréal, and as a new American consul took over that summer no special protection was provided at his house. That Cross himself noted this suggests he should perhaps have taken some precautions, but it was not his responsibility alone to assess the threat. He'd considered the possibility he could be a kidnapping target and then quickly rejected it with an almost prototypical humility of the British civil servant. He told the CBC in 1975 that the idea was unlikely because "I didn't think anyone would get anything for me."

The FLQ would think differently.

The members had rented an old apartment on Rue St. Jacques, and since there was no furniture, they slept in sleeping bags on the floor. They pinned up on the walls charts of figures, street addresses, schedules of about a dozen diplomats in the city. By their own admission in statements later, the FLQ had no intention of stopping with one kidnapping.

At first they wanted to start with the American diplomat, Burgess, but taking him presented logistical problems and higher risk. So they zeroed in on James "Jasper" Cross, whose function in the city as trade commissioner with Québec's supposed conquerors, whose clear vulnerability (Rose called him an easy target) and whose "Englishness" made him the perfect victim.

Calling their plan "Operation Liberation," they planned to demand the freeing of their comrades-in-arms, 23 people either charged or convicted of crimes ranging from manslaughter to kidnapping to armed robbery. These would come to be known as their "political prisoners."

But in September, there was a tactical disagreement that split the FLQ group into two factions. Lanctôt was eager to get on with kidnappings, while Paul Rose apparently didn't think their organization was strong enough yet. Rose and his supporters decided to go down to the U.S. to build up the group's war chest through a scheme involving traveller's cheque fraud. Lanctôt took charge of the operation that would kidnap Cross.

The night before James Cross found himself in a nightmarish ordeal, he was reading Graham Greene's *Travels With My Aunt* and ironically musing that like the novel's protagonist, his life had grown rather dull and staid. Just beyond his home on Redpath Crescent, one of the FLQ was keeping his house under surveillance.

The next morning, Cross puttered between his bathroom and his bedroom in only a shirt and his underpants as he discussed his busy week ahead with his wife. He was surprised to hear the doorbell so early, but his wife dismissed it as probably a man from Hydro Québec coming to read the meter. The strangers who came to his door were posing as deliverymen, and one shoved a gun in the face of the family's Portuguese maid. Within seconds, Cross was facing a handgun as one of his kidnappers told him, "Get down on the floor or you'll be fucking dead."

His head covered, taken away in handcuffs and forced to stay in a single room, Cross was convinced throughout most of his ordeal that he would be murdered by his captors.

Lanctôt later explained to their hostage his symbolic value. "We took Cross because he was the representative of England and Québec, because England is the mother country of Canada, and so by kidnapping James Cross, we were attacking the real symbol of colonial domination in Québec."

After hearing all this, Cross patiently replied, "My poor friends, I am actually Irish." Cross had been born in Ireland.

In addition to demanding the release of the 23 criminal prisoners, the FLQ also wanted the name of a presumed police informant, half-a-million dollars in gold, the police to call off their investigation into the kidnapping, safe passage to a foreign country such as Cuba or Algeria, and their latest manifesto read on television and published in newspapers.

Despite the news of the crime, Québec's 36-year-old premier, Robert Bourassa, who had been in power for only five months, went ahead with business as usual. He took a scheduled trip to New York. Ottawa was naturally involved since the kidnap victim was a member of the diplomatic community, and both the Secretary of State for External Affairs Mitchell Sharp and Bourassa's Justice Minister Jérôme Choquette took a hard line in their public statements.

Prime Minister Trudeau never wanted the FLQ's manifesto published and aired, but it was never really his choice. It had already received a limited hearing anyway when it was read on the French language radio station CKAC—*sans* government consent—and its text was in the hands of other media. Trudeau phoned up the executive vice-president of Radio Canada, Laurent Picard, who stood his ground over the network's journalistic autonomy. Mitchell Sharp, very much the old-fashioned Liberal from Winnipeg, who assumed reasonable people could see the manifesto as he and his colleagues saw it, disagreed with his boss and argued, "I think it would be a good thing for the people of Canada to see what these people are like."

The CBC anchor, Gaétan Montreuil, read the manifesto out in what came close to a monotone, which robbed it of what must have been intended as a shrill call to arms. It had been written in *joual*, Québec vernacular, and the style hit a chord with some as a clever tactic, but it was not an appeal with reasoned out arguments. "The *Front de Libération du Québec* wants total independence for Québeckers; it wants to see them united in a free society, a society purged for good of its gang of rapacious sharks, the big bosses who dish out patronage and their henchmen, who have turned Québec into a private preserve of cheap labour and unscrupulous exploitation...."

With its Marxist invective, the manifesto presumed its audience took the accusations as self-evident facts. Of course, many were familiar enough with the grievances and issues listed, from the Montréal taxi drivers' ongoing battle with the Murray Hill company to the brief strike by the city's police officers (before they were ordered back to work). "Workers of Québec, begin from this day forward to take back what is yours; take yourselves what belongs to you. Only you know your factories, your machines, your hotels, your universities, your unions; do not wait for some organization to produce a miracle."

Decades later, even the authorities conceded the manifesto had some rhetorical power. Jérôme Choquette called it "really punchy," and Trudeau considered its drafting "crude but clever." Trapped in an apartment on Avenue des Récollets with his head covered, James Cross heard his kidnappers' delighted joy over the manifesto being read.

A former member of Bourassa's cabinet, William Tetley, however, points out that there was no rushing to the ramparts. "There was no labour uprising or strike, let alone a general strike," he writes in *The October Crisis, 1970: An Insider's View*. "Students held meetings in their colleges and universities, but there were no demonstrations or marches in the streets, no riotous confrontations with police, no breaking of windows, no looting, no property damage, and no personal injury or arrests...it was only during the week following the kidnapping of Laporte that the meetings, demonstrations, and college and university closings started in earnest."

Bourassa's cabinet, like the federal one, had its own disagreements over how to respond to the kidnappers. Jérôme Choquette was a hawk from the beginning, and Tetley admits that at first he supported releasing the 23 criminal prisoners but soon changed his mind. Minister of Labour Pierre Laporte also took a strong stand, and Choquette recalled his colleague's disgust for those who wanted to give in to the FLQ. "A wind of folly is blowing over the province," quipped Laporte.

Choquette announced that if Cross was released unharmed, the kidnappers would be granted safe passage into exile from Canada. This may sound like a concession, but it was actually a tactical step. As Trudeau later outlined in a televised speech, allowing safe passage would take away any homicidal motive. After all, if the kidnappers were allowed out of the country, they had no reason to kill their hostages—these poor victims wouldn't need to help in any arrests or make any identification of suspects.

Twenty minutes after Choquette had made his statement, he was thunderstruck by a fresh development he learned from a reporter. There was word that an FLQ cell—which turned out to be the Chénier cell headed by Paul Rose—had snatched Pierre Laporte off his front lawn where he had been playing football with his nephew.

We will never know if Laporte changed his mind over his "no concessions" stance when he became a victim himself. The day after he was taken, a letter in his handwriting was released by his captors. It was addressed to the Québec premier, telling Bourassa that he held the "power of life or death" over him. Written under duress, it can't be taken for what Laporte actually thought or felt.

One of his young children wrote a letter to Bourassa that must have been equally, if not more, gut-wrenching for the young premier: "Please save my Daddy."

Bourassa moved his cabinet into a tightly guarded Queen Elizabeth Hotel in Montréal, while his ministers had to go about their business with police escorts. Many accounts and documentaries portray Bourassa and his government as panicking after the Laporte kidnapping. Tetley, who was there, disputes this, insisting Bourassa was calm.

Two days after Laporte was kidnapped, Trudeau ordered soldiers to guard public buildings and high-profile politicians in Ottawa. The presence of soldiers on the streets electrified the already tense atmosphere, and it led to one of the most famous confrontations in Canadian history. As Prime Minister Trudeau got out of his car in front of Centre Block on Parliament Hill, CBC reporter Tim Ralfe gently demanded, "Sir, what is it with all these men with guns around here?"

A smiling Trudeau at first appeared to joke away the question, asking, "Haven't you noticed?" And then, "What's your worry?" When Ralfe expressed concern, Trudeau turned the interrogation around by asking, "Have they done anything to you? Have they pushed you around or anything?"

Even today, our perceptions colour the moment. For an article on CBC's own website, radio producer Ira Basen claims Trudeau's voice was "dripping with sarcasm" as he fired these questions. Trudeau's voice actually wasn't sarcastic at all. The former law professor and skilled debater wasn't, however, about to let his opponent's position go unchallenged. He seemed genuinely interested in knowing if Ralfe had any substantial claims of abuse to back up his argument.

As the impromptu debate went on, Ralfe quietly hammered away, suggesting "one of the things I have to give up for that choice (to live in a democratic society) is the fact that people like you may be kidnapped." Trudeau replied it was more important to get rid of those who were committing violence against society and trying to run a parallel power.

Ralfe wasn't ready to concede the point, and Trudeau finally betrayed his irritation, snapping, "Yes, well there are a lot of bleeding hearts around who just don't like to see people with helmets and guns. All I can say is, go on and bleed, but it is more important to keep law and order in the society than to be worried about weak-kneed people who don't like the looks of—"

"At any cost?" broke in Ralfe. "How far would you go with that? How far would you extend that?"

Trudeau barely paused to consider his answer before replying, "Well, *just watch me.*"

Everyone did.

These three words were what made the most impact on the evening news, but the entire seven minutes of footage is riveting, even today. Noticeable, too, is the fact—so astonishingly quaint in our post 9/11 world—that the prime minister of the country had stepped out of his car with no impressive security detail around him, only Mounties in formal red uniforms standing ceremonial guard while representatives of the media were within less than an arm's reach.

As the Crisis rolled on, what was the English Canadian response? Sadly, today the CBC puts on its digital archive a clip from its 1970 radio program, *Double Take*, in which a female caller spouts drivel about how Francophones were privileged to be living in a "land of peace bought with English blood." She asks rhetorically how many Québecois were willing to fight in the Great War (ignoring the fact that conscription was used in Québec) and insisting the "Fatherland was calling us" (that is, England). She appeared unaware that some of the brightest minds born in the actual "Fatherland" and English Canadian war veterans all pointed out the futility of the conflict.

The CBC has labelled this clip, "Anglophone Rebuttal"—not *an* Anglophone Rebuttal; that is, one of a diverse range. The label suggests that this clip, with its ignorance and bizarre, out-of-touch Anglophile reverence were representative of English Canadian attitudes at the time. This amounts to a cheap trick of revisionism.

Although, no doubt, the FLQ's latest tactics were offered up in many an anti-French diatribe in households in the rest of the country, those hostile to the French and to Québec in particular were already sold on their prejudices. What repelled many English Canadians was the use of violence, whoever was using it. In major newspapers across Canada, there was understanding for the horrible pressure the provincial and federal governments were under.

Pierre Laporte's nephew had kept enough of a cool head to remember the licence plate of the car taking him away, and Paul Rose's fingerprint was typed from the first FLQ communiqué for the second kidnapping.

Which brings us back to the police finding their man at the Métro station—and then losing him. It begs the question: given the high stakes of this case, the unprecedented enormity of it, why didn't the officers watching the house have the good common sense to radio in for additional units to follow *anyone* who left?

The issue of how well the QPP and the Montréal police handled the Crisis is a matter for a different book, but the RCMP's role in the affair is very much in our scope. After all, it is the *Royal* Canadian Mounted Police—an organization that was very much, symbolically and in practical terms, an English institution.

It came out later that the RCMP and other police authorities did use informants to fight the FLQ, but it would be more than a decade before the security service of the Mounties was spun off and reorganized to become the Canadian Security Intelligence Service (CSIS). The RCMP, for instance, was a national police force always designed and equipped to deal with apprehending and charging suspects. As criminal as the FLQ was, it was a terrorist organization that required more sophisticated responses from a mature intelligence group that would have political insights.

The quintessentially "English" nature of the Mounties was such that they were still focusing on Marxist and Cold War enemies into the late '70s, ignoring the new potential threats emerging from multicultural terrorist groups that imported their feuds from abroad. Both the RCMP and the infant CSIS would come under heavy criticism for failing to prevent the bombing of Air India Flight 182 that departed Montréal in 1985.

As far as the October Crisis was concerned, even the RCMP's own Strategic Operation Centre would acknowledge eventually that it didn't have proper knowledge of the "Québec problem" and that it couldn't distinguish between the FLQ and separatism. The RCMP's failure was that of an English-influenced constabulary that was out of touch and out of date.

Bourassa's cabinet had its own reservations about how the police forces were handling the investigation. With the police taxed to their limits with hundreds of searches and with interviews of dozens of witnesses and suspects, one of the rationales for bringing the army into Montréal was so the police wouldn't be spread so thin. In dealing with the kidnappers through indirect negotiations, the province was willing to recommend parole for five of the criminals on the FLQ's list, and the promise of safe conduct out of Canada still stood. The FLQ lawyer Robert Lemieux rejected these offers (a government deadline for the hostages' release would trickle out, with no progress made and no response from the kidnappers).

Events were happening fast. Ontario's Premier John Robarts didn't just wade into the swirling rapids of the Crisis, but took a cannonball dive into them, telling the media, "We have to stand and fight. It's war—total war." Well, no, it wasn't. Such inflammatory language just added fodder for a petition distributed on October 14 to the media, one that had its own axe to grind and implied that forces beyond Québec would take advantage of the Crisis so the province would be "easy to keep under control." In other words, English Canada.

The petition was signed by 16 high-profile figures in Québec who came to be known as the "eminent personalities." They included René Lévesque and Jacques Parizeau of the PQ and Claude Ryan, editor and publisher of *Le Devoir*. The petitioners called for the hostages to be exchanged for the 23 criminal prisoners, ones they called "political prisoners," using the FLQ's language, and declared, "The Cross–Laporte affair is above all a Québec drama."

There were even rumours flying around Montréal that a provisional government could replace Bourassa's cabinet. Staff members of *Le Devoir* were apparently "flabbergasted" when their publisher Claude Ryan discussed the idea with them. A girlfriend of Jacques Parizeau at the time—she was an FLQ member and later a police informant—would later describe how he confided in her that certain individuals were ready to take over from the Bourassa cabinet, which was perceived as weak. To this day, the details of just who all these individuals were and how this scheme would have been carried out isn't quite known, but even in early November 1970, the premier was dismissive of the possibility.

Years later, Bourassa commented that he found the idea unrealistic. "Under the British system of government, to overthrow a government would have required a majority of the National Assembly. I had the loyalty of the Liberal Party." If others had abandoned the inherited concepts of English parliamentary law, the Québec premier had not.

Rumours were one thing. Something had changed with the kidnapping of Pierre Laporte. Students and a handful of teachers walked out of the Université de Montréal in support of the FLQ, and there were similar walkouts at a few of the junior colleges. If the FLQ had any residual doubts about popular sympathy among a part of the Québecois population, they got another measure of it when 3000 supporters, mostly students, packed into the Paul Sauvé Arena. They listened to speeches by Pierre Vallières, Charles Gagnon and Michel Chartrand, and they stood up and cheered after FLQ lawyer Robert Lemieux barked out in French, "We—will—win!" They exuberantly clapped and chanted, "FLQ, FLQ, FLQ!"

On October 15, the Québec government called in the army, and 7500 troops hit the streets of Montréal. Television is guilty most of all of blurring the lines and presenting the army and the War Measures Act as coming in at the same time. In fact, these were separate actions. As William Tetley points out, throughout the Crisis, soldiers could only exercise the same powers as the police, and they were still under civil authorities.

In one aspect, however, using the troops was a gamble for which Québec—and Trudeau as well—might have paid dearly if the violence had mushroomed. Back in 1970, the Canadian armed forces were English-dominated institutions with an Anglophone monopoly. Imagine if new FLQ cells had sprung up and committed fresh violence, with demonstrations growing in the streets? Inevitable confrontations would only lend credence to the twisted FLQ logic that English Canada was a colonial power "occupying" Québec.

But both Québec and Ottawa weren't about to let that happen. The next day, at the request of Premier Bourassa and Montréal Mayor Jean Drapeau, the Trudeau government imposed the War Measures Act. In the early morning hours of October 16, police swooped in and made dozens of arrests, a count that eventually reached close to 500 people. They didn't require search warrants, and under the Act, suspects could be held for up to 90 days.

Given the magnitude of the dragnet, there were bound to be mistakes and abuses. I know, personally, an individual who was arrested at the time while on a university campus. His offence? The police allegedly found the book he was carrying suspicious (it was, in fact, the required textbook for a political science course). The police even showed up at the Westmount front door of Gérard Pelletier, confusing the country's Secretary of State with a suspect of the same name.

The police arrested members of the Parti Québécois, but stopped short of hauling in its top leaders, such as René Lévesque and Jacques Parizeau. "We seem a little ridiculous," remarked Parizeau, "when our assistants are all arrested and not the big bosses."

As soldiers guarded the streets and police arrested scores of suspected FLQ members and sympathizers, order was gradually restored. Across the country, there was overwhelming support for bringing in the War Measures Act. True, much of Canada was reduced to looking on, and there were no soldiers grimly patrolling Moncton or Red Deer to spark debates over civil liberties, but it also has to be remembered that even in Québec, the majority were behind the move.

In the end, however, it was the FLQ who murdered its infant revolution in its cradle. They did it when members of the Chénier cell strangled Pierre Laporte and dumped his body in the trunk of a car only a day after the War Measures Act came in. At a large gathering organized by a Québecois civil liberties group, again made up of mostly students, the attendees broke into applause over the news of Laporte's "execution."

But this was an isolated incident. There was a wave of revulsion over the brutal murder, washing away the children's crusade atmosphere of students and would-be revolutionaries in Montréal. The FLQ's lawyer Robert Lemieux would later try in court to blame Laporte's death on Trudeau and the War Measures Act, but there is strong evidence that Laporte was strangled after he tried unsuccessfully to escape through a window, severely cutting himself.

René Lévesque was shocked by the murder as much as anyone else. Once the broadcaster who had to ask the tough questions in moments of drama and tragedy, he now faced an interviewer who wanted a 60-second clip of official PQ reaction. Off camera and still clearly upset, he told the reporter, "I don't want airtime, I couldn't care less about goddamn airtime. I'm not going to distort things... The guy dies, our opinion... aww, *shit!*"

When the camera started to roll, Lévesque took a deep breath and, put on the spot, rambled about how the terrorists had no "sense of humanity who don't reflect Québec." But he then went on to suggest once more that Ottawa and the Bourassa government should make concessions to the FLQ, and that Ottawa shared responsibility for

Laporte's death (then he suggested the kidnappers give up). "But on the other hand, let no one think wherever he is—outside Québec or inside Québec—that this is enough to make us a sort of cell, a collective cell of repression. We'll fight if we have to against anyone who wants to use this climate now, to more or less, you know, tie up Québec in impotence."

The media now speculated whether James Cross was still alive, and Cross himself was stuck in a chair in his kidnappers' hideout, watching TV and horrified by what his wife was probably thinking. He recalled years later in a taped memoir, "I wanted to get up and shake the television set and scream, 'I'm not dead! I'm not dead!'" His ordeal would go on for almost another two months of alternating dread and banal routine.

The whole saga still had plenty of bizarre twists to baffle everyone involved. Police captured Bernard Lortie of the Chénier cell in a Queen Mary Road apartment, but they missed others hiding behind a false wall in a closet. The others slipped away the next day through a back door.

Time, of course, was always on the side of the plodding, unrelenting investigation. The police knew who many of the kidnappers were; they had their names and faces. Those who killed Laporte were now on the run, while the members holding Cross had become captives, themselves, of their own situation.

On the night of December 2, the FLQ members holding Cross felt an eerie quiet in the apartment above theirs on Avenue des Récollets. Their instinct was right—the police had them surrounded, and they soon shut off the power. The kidnappers decided to write a letter for the police and throw it out the window in a steel pipe. As they drafted their note, Cross remembered one of them suggesting the FLQ slogan, "We Will Win," be added. Everyone, even the hostage, "burst out laughing."

The kidnappers wired the door with explosives and had to dismantle them the next morning when negotiations began. Finally, in the early afternoon, a car made its way through a gauntlet of hundreds of police and soldiers on the way to the site of Expo '67 (temporarily designated the Cuban Consulate), carrying the kidnappers (still armed with dynamite) and their hostage. One of the vehicle's back doors was shaky, and Cross—worried Jacques Lanctôt might fall out—hung on to him. As the kidnappers left on a plane for Cuba, Cross spoke to his relieved wife in Switzerland and was pleased that Jérôme Choquette had the presence of mind to show up bringing along a couple of bottles of wine and a corkscrew.

On December 28, police found Paul Rose, his brother Jacques and Francis Simard of the Chénier cell hiding in a 20-foot tunnel under a furnace in a house in Saint-Luc, not far from Montréal.

It's been a case of serial epilogues for the October Crisis ever since. Both Paul Rose and Francis Simard, for example, were sentenced to life imprisonment, but both were walking around free by 1982. After four trials over his part in the Laporte murder, Jacques Rose was freed conditionally in 1978. Those that had fled to Cuba eventually returned to face Canadian justice, but they received light sentences because their time in exile was factored in. Jacques Lanctôt was given one year in prison for kidnapping Cross.

In the wake of an inquiry by the Québec provincial government 10 years after the Crisis, a mysterious British-born engineering student, Nigel Hamer—almost completely forgotten, going on about his life—was arrested and pled guilty for his role in the kidnapping of James Cross. He spent only a few months in prison.

The FLQ's lawyer Robert Lemieux spent his remaining career championing labour union and Aboriginal claims. In its obituary for him, *The Gazette* suggested he had become "a pariah in Montréal legal circles" that defended members of the Hell's Angels biker gang, whom he called "more or less political prisoners."

And what of the surviving kidnap victim? He would return to Canada a few more times, once as a guest of a memorial mass for Pierre Laporte. I was told in 1996, by one of Cross' friends and a fellow trade official, that after the shaken victim returned to Britain, his superiors tactlessly suggested, "Well, of course, you're going back." A shocked Cross replied something to the effect that, of course, he would do no such thing.

Cross was, according to this friend, similarly dismayed by the rather ham-fisted manner in which British authorities did all they could to prevent him from telling his story to the media (he was getting lucrative offers, some as high as £100,000). He was clearly bitter about his treatment by his own government, reporting in his taped memoir years later that Britain's Foreign Office "which had done very little to aid me in my captivity had been very effective in blocking any gain by me and had already consulted the Civil Service department and the Cabinet Office and a firm veto was in place."

The debate over the War Measures Act still goes on, and William Tetley still tries to correct misconceptions and lack of knowledge of the facts. He points out that contrary to popular belief, the Act didn't suspend all civil liberties. While the government banned the FLQ, students and political parties were still free to meet and criticize the government's actions throughout the Crisis. This was, you'll remember, how students were able to gather and cheer Laporte's murder when the news came through.

Of more than 200 complaints over detention under the War Measures Act, Québec ombudsman Louis Marceau found in 1971 that less than half had merit and deserved compensation.

The War Measures Act is today often confused as being Canada's own version of martial law, but this was hardly the case—not even close. Martial law implies generals were running the show, and that didn't happen in the Montréal of 1970. Let me add a personal aside here. In 2005, I lived and worked, teaching journalism for a brief time, in Myanmar (Burma), a country *really* under martial law. I spoke to reporters who were blatantly threatened by army generals, I met individuals tossed into detention who were tortured, and I worked for a newspaper that was censored on a daily basis. Ordinary people are often restricted in their travel in and out of the country and have trouble obtaining ordinary passports. It's a nation that has had actual martial law since 1962, not months. Its people live in a constant state of fear.

Compare that to the Canada of 1970, where the government actually set up a Committee to Aid Persons Arrested Under the War Measures Act, where the federal government itself took the initiative to bring in the Public Order (Temporary Measures) Act in early November to replace the heavy club it had been wielding. Reporters were not routinely intimidated and threatened, people were free to travel, and the general population mostly supported the government's response.

In December 1981, a bearded Jacques Rose stood before the throng of a Parti Québécois convention and got a standing ovation. René Lévesque looked on, his shaking head falling into his hands in dismay. As late as 2000, Francis Simard and Paul Rose could be treated as honoured guests at a meeting in Montréal of old members of the *Rassemblement pour l'Indépendance Nationale*, a separatist group that was absorbed into the PQ. Ironically, some of the most vocal opponents against the War Measures Act in the historical debate today were members of the FLQ—people who were responsible for starting the Crisis in the first place!

And as William Tetley points out, they have the gall to complain about the use of force by the democratic system they wanted to overthrow.

Trudeau understood this all too well—it was the reason he didn't want to give the terrorists "publicity" or a platform. But the issue goes even deeper. The FLQ wanted it both ways: to wage violence yet carry on a political and a historical debate. It was not simply trying to be a parallel power but to win hearts and minds on the parallel track of the very English tradition for which it held contempt. Debate in a legislature and in a free press has its roots in an English tradition, one that was kept and refined by the American revolutionaries, and which took time to be reborn in France after its revolution imploded and after the fall of Napoleon, that great betrayer of the revolutionaries' ideals. When former FLQ members criticized the suspension of civil liberties years later, they conveniently forgot, in diatribes against English oppression, that habeas corpus is a tradition that stems from English law.

In fact, the Habeas Corpus Act was passed in 1679 during the reign of that enemy of New France we're already familiar with, Charles II. And its main champion was a member of the first committee of the Hudson's Bay Company, the Earl of Shaftesbury.

I did mention early in this book that history has a habit of coming back and knocking on the door like a bill collector.

Such nuances wouldn't have mattered at all to those 3000 supporters who chanted in the Paul Sauvé Arena. Caught up in their revolutionary feeling, they forgot to think—to remember that two innocent men had been kidnapped, including one of their own fellow Québecois, and that others were murdered in bank robberies, slain or maimed by bombs. If you devalued the victims then or do so in today's revision of history ("Oh, but in those times…"), you are granting licence to devalue everybody.

It takes nothing away from the legitimate grievances of the Québecois in 1970 to argue that those who were sympathetic or played apologist for the FLQ were following a completely different tradition, a European one that inspired a romanticist pipe-dream of "violence chic." It's the image of the underdog artist, the warrior idyll that expresses itself in Hugo's *Les Misérables* and in the Paris Commune, and that has found its way onto thousands of Che Guevara T-shirts. Anglo Canada, of course, has had the flip side of this in every misty-eyed and uninformed, jingoistic recollection of rushing off to fight for dear ol' England, a nostalgia chilled by the reality of concentration camps in the Boer War and the battle of the Somme.

In discussing the War Measures Act in *A Military History of Canada*, Desmond Morton declares, "On the basis of facts then and revealed later, it was unjustified." But this is hindsight. It insists the FLQ never had more than a collection of diehard members. The truth was that the government had reason to fear sympathizers would and did aid and abet the hardcore, and that more would be recruited. They were looking at more than just two kidnappings—they had experienced seven years of terrorist violence. But Morton goes on to call the invocation of the Act a "brilliant success," and because he writes it so much more eloquently, let him sum up the effect:

"Shock was the best safeguard against bloodshed. Trudeau's target was not two frightened little bands of terrorists, one of which soon strangled its helpless victim: it was the affluent dilettantes of revolutionary violence, cheering on the anonymous heroes of the FLQ. The proclamation of the War Measures Act and the thousands of grim troops pouring into Montréal froze the cheers, dispersed the coffee-table revolutionaries and left them frightened and isolated while the police rounded up suspects, whose offence, if any, was dreaming of blood in the streets."

In fact, "psychological shock" was the term the Trudeau government itself used privately for the troops going in and for the use of the War Measures Act.

And this result is why Canada is the way it is today.

We have lived, as a country, in the shadow of a helmet and rifle on Parliament Hill ever since. It doesn't matter anymore whether bleeding hearts "go on and bleed" or if supportive, even occasionally spiteful cheers well up from a prairie field or a Maritime fishing dock. When people considered both the grisly murder of Laporte, and those troops on the street, it was no longer a question of what Québec was or what Canada was. We collectively decided then—English and French Canada both—that we did not want to be Argentina or Chile. We didn't want to be England either, regularly paralyzed by IRA attacks at the time, or France, where de Gaulle *had* sent in the tanks to quell student rebellion two years earlier.

When it comes down to it, we debate the invocation of the War Measures Act not because it was the right or wrong thing to do, but because the extremes of terrorism and the suspension of civil liberties, even if temporarily needed and justified, are so contrary to our national character—both English *and* French identities. The decision started with the Bourassa cabinet, but Trudeau became the voice that made it bluntly clear: if this is what you truly want, this is what you will get in response—a state unapologetically defending itself.

The Battle of Vimy Ridge was not our "coming of age"; October 1970 was. People woke up from a nightmare of a Canada pushed to its limits to realize that, in everyday life, there is no shred of nobility in manning barricades and taking lives when we have the functional, if less "glamorous" alternative of democratic representation. We grew up as a country that year, and arguably, this is really where our image to the rest of the world as a peaceful, law-abiding and tolerant nation begins—not for the absence of global headlines over such violence, but because this political violence is anathema to us. Canada will not be *that* place.

Jérôme Choquette understood this point when he gave his opinion of how the Crisis affected Québec society. Speaking to journalist Terence McKenna in 2000 for the documentary, *Black October*, he said, "I think it purged us of the violence that prevailed at that time. People became conscious of the dangers of violence. They had it, and they had proof of it, what it had resulted in. And they disapproved of any violent action, and I think it permitted then much more civil discussion of political differences that we have been living with for now maybe 25 or 30 years."

If the seemingly endless dialogue to resolve English–French differences has often numbed Canadians into a torpor, if Meech Lake and the Charlottetown Accord made us all shake our heads in frustration, we can be buoyed by the fact that we are still talking. The alternative is too horrific to contemplate. We got a bitter taste of it and were mercifully spared. The Québec referendums of 1980 and 1995, regardless of their outcomes, were reaffirmations of democracy by the very fact that they were held at all.

LEGACIES: AND JUST HOW IS "MOTHER" DOING? (AS IN ENGLAND)

The Old Country, meanwhile, had lifted its head out of the rubble of World War II and realized there was no going back. India wanted, once and for all, out of the Empire. So did Burma. Then Ghana, Kenya, and the trickle of countries ready to be on their own became a flood. The old joke of a newspaper headline once went: "Fog in Channel, Continent Cut Off." In the 1960s, the U.K. recognized its economic survival could well depend on becoming part of a European continent, an argument that goes on to this day.

Canada was also changing through this time, and English Canada had to come to grips with more than just the way it treated Francophones. Aboriginal peoples and those in Afro–Caribbean communities were losing their patience with the marginalizing, indifference and outright racism they faced in a Canada that patted itself on the back as a country morally superior to its southern neighbour.

To walk down the streets of Regina and Winnipeg in January was to see clusters of homeless Natives sleeping on the cold pavement—many were doomed to freeze to death. In Halifax in the 1950s, black people were forced to sit in the balconies of movie theatres, a notorious practice we normally associate with America. And then there was Africville, a community on the edge of Halifax bordered by railway tracks, an abattoir and a dump, where the residents were denied trash pickup, water and electricity—yet were still charged taxes for services. ✓

It's English Canada who has to answer primarily for this past. Yes, change did come—but slowly. It came thanks to activists taking their cue from the civil rights struggles south of the border. It also came from the Liberal strategy to defeat the separatists: multiculturalism. Under the new doctrine, no single people defined Canada, every culture could. The magic word taught in schools was *mosaic;* nobody had to "melt" into a pot as was expected of Americans. Canadians, both English ones and those from elsewhere, definitely liked the sound of that—it spoke to our quiet individualism instead of the herd patriotic fervour of the U.S. that has so often rubbed us the wrong way.

Back in the land with centuries more history but much less space, the English had—and still have—more trouble adapting to the new multicultural world. There has always been a myth that somehow the English were more tolerant in terms of race than Americans and perhaps even Canadians. This is rubbish. In 1948, the *Empire Windrush* brought over about 500 immigrants from Jamaica eager to work and begin new lives in the United Kingdom. It was the start of something, and more

Caribbean citizens and later people from India arrived. The insular, reactionary segments of the white population, horrified they might actually have to live side by side with their former colonial subjects, often refused them jobs and houses. By the late 1950s, racist gangs and "Teddy Boys" were attacking West Indians on the street and vandalizing their homes, which culminated in the Notting Hill riots.

One year after Canada celebrated the multicultural extravaganza that was Expo '67, across the Atlantic, Conservative MP Enoch Powell shocked Britain with his views on where the country was going in terms of race. "Like the Roman, I seem to see 'the River Tiber foaming with much blood.'" (Powell was a Classics scholar. The image was so inflammatory that his address became known as the Rivers of Blood Speech.) In denouncing immigration, Powell quoted what were clearly racist constituents of his riding, including one who told him "in 15 or 20 years time the black man will have the whip hand over the white man." The Conservative leader Edward Heath sacked him, but Powell had thousands of supporters, including rocker Eric Clapton, who claims to this day Powell couldn't have been a racist.

Awareness gradually evolved in England, but there was sometimes a shocking lack of sensibilities compared to how its former Canadian colony was doing. The number one show on British television from 1957 right until 1978, believe it or not, was *The Black and White Minstrel Show*. It was exactly what it sounds like: Welsh singers in blackface. "Now imagine if you're me growing up here," a British African friend told me, "and that's on every week."

In terms of economics, Britain—and specifically London—was still a financial powerhouse and remains one to this day, but we might wonder if we're better off here in terms of our own financial affairs. Stats Canada says most of us live under the pleasant delusion we're middle class, even when we're not. In England, this is still impossible. Contrary to what you might think or see on *EastEnders*, there hasn't been a genuine Cockney accent in London for decades, but there linger scores of local accents that announce where you're from and what tier you're on. You can be stunned to hear the anachronistic "Guv" still used by English clerks at veggie markets and shoe repairers of the Timpsons chain. Class still matters. Money always matters.

In Canada, most of our millionaires know enough not to stir our envy. They keep a fairly low profile—it took Peter C. Newman to let us know who made up the Canadian Establishment. In England, you can never forget. You are well aware of who has and will have the power, the title and the money. Boys at the Harrow school still wear the signature straw boater hat, and when you walk into a conference at the Institute of Directors on Pall Mall, the gilt frames, statues and lush surroundings can overwhelm you. Power meets money here, right next to famous gentlemen's clubs, still open today and just up the road from the Queen's house.

Appearance is everything, and of course, it can be deceiving. I learned this firsthand when I was editing a business magazine in the heart of London's financial district, known as "The City." To get promotional articles written, the banks and investment houses were happy to bribe me with lunch at places I could never afford to go on my own. I was nothing; they wanted the magazine's key slots. So I sat under crystal chandeliers, enjoying great meals on someone else's tab three days out of five. I was paid well, but not very well, so that we lived at the time in the South Asian–dominated suburb of Harrow called Wealdstone. ✐

One weekend afternoon, I answered the door to find a group of smiling, white Christian charity workers shoving the equivalent of a care package into my arms, saying, "This is for *you!*" I told them I work, my partner worked—we didn't need it. No, no, they assured me, they were handing out packages like this all along the block. Their smiles were beatific, and they were so pleased with themselves for rescuing all of us.

I shrugged and thought, oh, well, free food. It never occurred to them to notice in front of the cracked streets and rundown houses the row of Mercedes and BMWs belonging to my neighbours from India and Pakistan. The care package turned out to be a disappointment—the Christians apparently assumed we impoverished wretches ate crap—they had included powdered mashed potato mix and canned Spam. Up the street, you could buy lovely kebabs and tasty, healthy Indian takeaways at cheaper prices than these groceries. Still, this episode was quite the education. In the City, I ate with bankers. At home, I was identified as a charity case.

But it is arguably far easier to navigate the ladders of race and class in England than it's ever been, even if there are still those sawing away at the rungs. England has stayed in its museum glass case for the lucrative tourist trade while embracing change in other ways. It is a land of cell phones—"mobiles"—a land already ahead of us in banning talking on your cell while you drive, a place where Heritage buildings are strongly protected yet one that's resigned to scrapping thousands of the famous red call boxes. England is the land with the most CCTV surveillance in the world. For better or worse, someone from the comparatively recent time of Beaverbrook wouldn't recognize England today.

Maybe this is why so many of us reacted with derision when Conrad Black wrapped himself in ermine robes and became a lord. He wanted to join the other mummified sleepwalkers in a redlined chamber that represents a dead past.

But then our relationship with England has always been one of messy family politics. The child wants independence but also seeks recognition, approval. The absentee parent is not easily impressed and often reacts with galling indifference. As you walk into Trafalgar Square, once and forever one of the most important spots in London, you see *our* embassy, the Canadian High Commission. It's in a beautiful and grand building. Right behind it on Cockspur Street, just to bring you humbly back down to Earth, is the "Texas Embassy"—a Tex–Mex restaurant. When you watch the British Parliament on television, you see the two sides debate on a table that was a gift from Canada after German planes bombed the original House of Commons. Most Canadians don't know this. Most English don't care.

While living in the U.K., I ran into my fair share of English people who sometimes teased me, sometimes were quite serious in dismissing Canada as a place of few accomplishments, a dull land not worth visiting. Like a stand-up comic dealing with hecklers, I developed the best response to torpedo this condescension. Go ahead and ignore us, I replied, *please* do. We have the largest reserves of fresh water in the world, vast forests of timber, riches in minerals we haven't even begun to mine and oh, yes, land—*lots* of it. Let's see now, how big is your tiny little island filling up with 80 million people and counting? Good luck with those dwindling resources and the localized effects of global warming. ✓

In our best moments, however, the connection stays affectionate and strong. As I mentioned in the Introduction, John Keegan recognized that the English today bring attitudes to Canada—but they can change. In ways small and grand, our interest in how the parent is doing hasn't diminished. The Queen and her family still make news with a visit. The revitalized *Doctor Who* episodes we see rebroadcast in Canada are not entirely an import—they were partially funded by the CBC.

We've become a nation of contradictions as well. We import many good shows of British television, faithfully watching them on CBC or PBS, yet with the flood of American shows, we imitate—sometimes to excruciatingly embarrassing degrees—our neighbours to the south.

But on television and radio, as well as in print, we do humour well, and our brand of humour is our own—absurd, surreal, pointed but not cruel. Watching a touring Canadian perform in a comedy club in Wembley Park, my partner turned and whispered to me, "So you're *all* like this!" Yes, I suppose we are, but England helped make us this way. It's difficult to trace the comedy genealogy, but Canadians were fans of Monty Python years before the Americans "discovered" the troupe. Canadians know *Blackadder* and *Yes, Prime Minister*, and older ones know who Spike Milligan was. There is a debt of inspiration.

Our literature naturally owes much to England, and you can find Canadian writers from Robertson Davies to Mordecai Richler who lived there and felt its influence. Just as Canadian film and journalism has its roots in England. John Grierson, the father of both the British and the Canadian documentary, was, of course, a Scot. But he surrounded himself with a group of pioneering English filmmakers like Humphrey Jennings and Basil Wright, and certainly Grierson's battles with the thoroughly English bureaucracy of the Empire Marketing Board informed his opinion of how Canada should organize its film production.

The connection goes deeper—to a reserved, English way of covering current events (and we're talking about the papers and networks of record here, not the London tabloid tradition that offers half-naked Page Three girls and retractions every other day). It's a subjective point, but to watch Fox or CBS News or to read the *New York Times* is to always get the *American* view; Canadian correspondents at least try for objectivity and the perspective of the culture being reported on. We are an enormous country, and yet we look outward. American networks have the money, but they complain their own reporters prefer to stay at home. We'll go to Bosnia for them. We'll go to Rwanda. And it can't be coincidence that the one other people to first send out an army of curious correspondents around the world happened to be the English through the BBC.

And then there is the unfinished business of the monarchy and our ties to it. We don't seem to be quite done with the royals yet, and some of us can still act "more English than the English." Our most imperious of governors general, Adrienne Clarkson, the first Chinese Canadian to hold the post and a devout Anglican, felt obliged to condescendingly point out in her book, *Heart Matters*, how the Queen Mother used different china settings at a formal dinner. As if anyone gives a damn. As for Clarkson, Canadians have reaffirmed their position that they're happy to have a Queen's representative, just not one who insists on behaving and spending our money as if she were the Queen.

As England evolves, so do we, having taken from it the best and a bit of the worst, but reshaping those influences into an exciting character of our own. Looking back on how England helped create Canada, we should be impressed with the tangible accomplishments of both this founding people and Canadians. History is the best antidote to the Hamlet-esque navel gazing we've engaged in for more than 30 years, asking what we are and if we'll survive as a country in a steady tide of soon-to-be remaindered analysis books and dreary news segments. Far better to look at all the English did and what we have done. A national identity doesn't rest on rationalizations or academic debate. It needs a vigorous will. It needs emotional bonds and a view both forward and backward.

The panorama behind us of great peoples creating this country—First Nations, French, African and Afro–Caribbean, Scottish, so many others and, of course, the English—should remind us we have always been steering toward a brilliant destiny.

NOTES ON PRIMARY SOURCES

Anderson, Fred. *Crucible of War.* New York: Knopf, 2000.

Brumwell, Stephen. *Paths of Glory: The Life and Death of General James Wolfe.* Montreal & Kingston: McGill-Queen's University Press, 2006.

Cook, Tim. *At the Sharp End: Canadians Fighting the Great War 1914–1918.* Toronto: Penguin Canada, 2007.

Cooper, Leonard. *Radical Jack: The Life of John George Lambton.* London: Cresset Press, 1959.

Creighton, Donald. *John A. Macdonald: The Young Politician, The Old Chieftain.* Toronto: University of Toronto Press, 1998 reprint.

Gilmour, Don, Achille Michaud, and Pierre Turgeon. *A People's History of Canada, Volumes One and Two.* Toronto: McClelland & Stewart, 2000.

Hickey, Donald R. *Don't Give Up the Ship! Myths of the War of 1812.* Toronto: Robin Brass Studio, 2006.

Hoy, Claire. *Canadians in the Civil War.* Toronto: McArthur & Company, 2004.

Jobb, Dean. *The Acadians: A People's Story of Exile and Triumph.* Toronto: John Wiley & Sons Canada, 2005.

Keegan, John. *Fields of Battle: The Wars for North America.* New York: Knopf, 1996.

Kelly, William, and Nora Kelly. *The Royal Canadian Mounted Police: A Century of History.* Edmonton: Hurtig Publishers, 1973.

Latimer, John. *1812: War with America*. London: Belknap Press, 2007.

Morton, Desmond. *A Military History of Canada*. 5th ed. Toronto: McClelland & Stewart, 2007.

Mitchell, Leslie. *Bulwer Lytton: The Rise and Fall of a Victorian Man of Letters*. London: Hambledon and London, 2003.

Newman, Peter C. *Empires of the Bay*. Toronto: Penguin edition, 1998.

Paxman, Jeremy. *The English*. London: Penguin, 1999.

Poitras, Jacques. *Beaverbrook: A Shattered Legacy*. Fredericton: Goose Lane Editions, 2007.

Scobie, Edward. *Black Britannia: A History of Blacks in Britain*. Chicago: Johnson Publishing, 1972.

Silcox, David P. *The Group of Seven and Tom Thomson*. Toronto: Firefly Books, 2006.

Tetley, William. *The October Crisis, 1970: An Insider's View*. Montreal & Kingston: McGill-Queen's University Press, 2007.

Walker, JamesW. St. G. *The Black Loyalists: The Search for a Promised Land in Nova Scotia and Sierra Leone, 1783–1870*. Toronto: University of Toronto Press, reprinted edition, 1999.

Williams, Jeffery. *Byng of Vimy: General and Governor General*. London: Leo Cooper, 1983.

Zuehlke, Mark. *For Honour's Sake: The War of 1812 and the Brokering of an Uneasy Peace*. Toronto: Vintage Canada edition, 2007.

"Canada the peacekeeper? A myth that should die" by Sunil Ram:http://www.theglobeandmail.com/servlet/story/RTGA.20040825.w/BNStory/Front/

JEFF PEARCE

Jeff Pearce has worked as a writer and editor for both television and magazines. He lived in the UK for six years, mostly in the Greater London area, where he examined the English close up and developed a shrewd understanding of English culture. In 2005, he taught journalism in Myanmar (Burma), a country where reporters are routinely harassed and often imprisoned. He has had eight novels published in the UK and the U.S. and has won several awards for his fiction. His play, *Defenders of Gravity,* won out over more than 100 scripts to inaugurate the first "Playwrights of Spring" festival held at Theatre Aurora in Ontario.